# The Narrow Road

## A Catholic's Path to Spiritual Growth

B Jeffrey Anderson
2014

In Association with
Regnum Dei Press
RegnumDeiPress.com

Copyright © 2014 by B. Jeffrey Anderson
All rights reserved.


Nihil Obstat:
    Daniel Burke.
    Censor Librorum Deputatis

Imprimatur:
    Most Reverend Robert J. Baker, S.T.D.
    Bishop of Birmingham in Alabama
    June 27, 2014


Unless otherwise noted, Scripture texts in this work are taken from the *New American Bible, revised edition* © 2010, 1991, 1986, 1970 Confraternity of Christian Doctrine, Washington, D.C. and are used by permission of the copyright owner. All Rights Reserved. No part of the New American Bible may be reproduced in any form without permission in writing from the copyright owner.

Scripture texts identified as NIV are from THE HOLY BIBLE, NEW INTERNATIONAL VERSION®, NIV® Copyright © 1973, 1978, 1984, 2011 by Biblica, Inc.® Used by permission. All rights reserved worldwide.

Quotes are taken from the English translation of the *Catechism of the Catholic Church* for the United States of America (indicated as *CCC with the paragraph number*), 2nd ed. © 1997 by United States Catholic Conference—Libreria Editrice Vaticana.


ISBN: 1500480541
ISBN-13: 978-1500480547

# Dedication

*Dedicated to Bob and Gai, Mom and Dad, and the many others whose courage and positive response to God contributed so greatly to helping me find the narrow road.*

# Contents

|     | Foreword | vii |
|-----|----------|-----|
|     | Acknowledgments | ix |
|     | Introduction | 1 |
| 1.  | The Narrow Gate | 5 |
| 2.  | A Vision of the Kingdom | 17 |
| 3.  | Service, the Kingdom, and the Cross | 27 |
| 4.  | Sin and the Sacraments | 35 |
| 5.  | Ruts in the Road | 47 |
| 6.  | Let the Journey Begin | 57 |
| 7.  | Guidance and Discernment | 67 |
| 8.  | Traveling in the HOV Lane | 83 |
| 9.  | Out of the Desert | 95 |
| 10. | Closing Notes | 107 |
|     | About the Author | 111 |

# Foreword

Pope Francis said[1], "Jesus tells us that there is a door to enter into the family of God. This door is Jesus." Jesus through his life, death, and resurrection offers himself as the way of salvation for all. "Everyone is invited to enter this door, to go through the door of faith, to enter into His life, and to allow Jesus into their lives, so that he may transform them, renew them, and give them full and lasting joy."

The Pope went on to say there are many doors that deceive, "inviting us to enter, promising instant happiness, which is an end in itself and has no future." However, Jesus "shines a light in our lives that never goes out. It is more than just a flash."

We are encouraged to not be afraid to enter the door of faith in Jesus. We must not be afraid "to let him enter more and more into our lives, to get us out of our selfishness, our being closed off, our indifference towards others."

This way of Jesus is "narrow" because "he asks us to open our heart to him, to recognize ourselves as sinners in need of his salvation, his forgiveness, his love, and to have the humility to accept his mercy and let us be renewed by him." It is also narrow because of the world's deception; our culture attempts to hide the path with half-truths and false blessings.

Jeff Anderson was not afraid to embrace Pope Francis' Catholic Church ideology and has addressed these and many other dimensions of our journey with the Lord in this book. Most importantly, he clearly shows the markers, the road signs, which the Lord has given to keep us on the proper path, the path which is a special call to each

---

[1] Angelus audience on August 25, 2013.

person leading to a unique place in God's family. He specifically invites each of us to look at the ways in which we have been touched by the Holy Spirit and are actively being guided by Jesus.

This book shows how taking up our role as God's servants is the key to closer communication with Jesus and the experience of being baptized in the Holy Spirit. Openness to the Spirit manifests a fuller living of the Gospel evident in and through us. The gifts of communication and discernment help us navigate through the narrow door that Pope Francis talks about. Testimony from Jeff's personal life gives us a gentle reminder that the challenges of living the Gospel that the Pope speaks of are to be sought by all, and for all who seek, the graces of the encounter are available in abundance.

—Jane Guenther, M.Div.

>Chairman of the Catholic Charismatic Renewal National Service Committee,

>Director of the Catholic Renewal Center for the Archdiocese of St. Louis

# Acknowledgements

*What a joy, when working on a large project, to have person after person step forward and contribute their wisdom, time, and encouragement. In particular I must acknowledge Elfrena S Foord for her encouragement, organizational skill, and wisdom that started me in the right direction. Encouragement and many excellent suggestions came from reviewers of the early drafts: Deborah Anderson, Fr. Joy Chalissery, and especially the detailed and critical reviews by Mr. Al Mansfield and Deacon James Bodine. Absolutely excellent editorial support was provided by Claudia Volkman and Ruth Johnson, with proof checking by Sheila Weigel. To each of them I am deeply indebted and grateful. Through it all I was blessed by the wisdom and support of my wife Beth; Proverbs 31:10-31 describes her well.*

*Cover designed in conjunction with Jan Kwit–Conklin of Denver, CO.*

# Introduction

*Enter through the narrow gate; for the gate is wide and the road broad that leads to destruction, and those who enter through it are many. How narrow the gate and constricted the road that leads to life. And those who find it are few. Matt 7:13-14*

The sign said it clearly enough: "Next Services 83 Miles." My wife and I had already traveled the better part of an hour without seeing significant signs of civilization on that afternoon in early March, and the day was growing late. The scenery was the beautiful desolation of the Utah-Nevada border country. Another sign and more pause for thought: "No Maintenance in Winter." My cell phone read, "Searching for Service." We didn't expect to see much traffic on that section of highway, and we didn't: one pickup truck, two sets of wide-load escort vehicles, and a heavy-duty wrecker. Off to the side of the road there was a police vehicle and two semi-trucks that had been pulling sections of a mobile home.

The actual distance to Ely, Nevada, and the first services we actually encountered was about 144 miles. That's why we stopped briefly just before sunset to talk with a man sitting in an SUV near the side of the road. We didn't want to be stuck out there at night, and I didn't want anyone else to be, either. We discovered that he was waiting for the already overdue wide loads so he could direct them to the proper location. From what we had seen, we told him they wouldn't be along any time soon, certainly not before dark. The man was visibly relieved because we had stopped; now he understood the situation and knew what to do.

I relate this little incident to explain the purpose of this book. This book is intended to be a helpful guide to spiritual growth, and in many ways searching for spiritual growth is like traveling along that

*Introduction*

road which was smooth, yet desolate and uncertain. On such a journey even the friendly wave of a stranger is welcome and brings comfort. The Lord, through Scripture and the Church, strives to provide a smooth, mostly straight, well-marked road, but as our Lord reminds us in Matthew's passage above, the road is also "constricted" ("narrow" or "rough" in other translations). Certainly the journey is often very solitary, and many difficulties and unexpected events can and do occur. On the one hand, it does not take long to identify Jesus as the narrow gate, the point of entry. On the other, just as Paul warned, "at present we see indistinctly, as in a mirror" (1 Cor. 13:12). Secular culture and the human condition tend to cause a certain distortion of the truth which, like the poor quality of the mirrors of Paul's day, makes it difficult for us to fully perceive and embrace the truths we need for spiritual growth. My wife Beth and I have traveled that road for some decades now, and we have seen and learned a lot. I can't map out the difficulties that lie ahead for you, but I can give you the benefit of my experience. Hopefully what we share will provide confidence, bring ideas on how to cope, and help you move smoothly and quickly toward a deep spiritual relationship with Jesus.

This book is not intended to be a deep or complete treatise on spiritual growth; rather, it is something of a travelogue for beginners, pointing out where to go and what to watch for spiritually. If you are a young mother struggling to get in a single decade of the Rosary while nursing your baby, a breadwinner who says his morning prayer in the midst of a traffic jam on the way to work, a student still trying to figure out how to get your prayers answered, this book is for you. With God's grace, it will help bring you to the point where you are a bearer of good fruit and ready to sit at the feet of the great masters of the spiritual life the Church has blessed us with: St. Thérèse of Lisieux, St. Teresa of Avila, St. John of the Cross, Brother Lawrence, and Ignatius of Loyola, among others.

*Introduction*

Of course, the reality is that the lessons necessary for effective spiritual growth have been around a long time, certainly long before me, available to everyone in the teaching of Scripture, the Church, and the saints. But the Lord has not been idle in our generation, and the issues and understanding of our current culture changes and evolves. Thus, the focus of this book is clarity for the modern reader, encouragement, faith, and courage. It is also, in a very direct sense, a book on down-in-the-pew Church renewal—renewal in the sense of removing the faulty perception of the Church's truth that inhibits the growth of so many Catholics. Individual spiritual growth and Church renewal go hand in hand. The struggle for spiritual growth may seem to be a lonely and very personal struggle, but it is the Church that marks the road and then provides the sustenance that carries us forward. The faithful laity are the core of the Church, and as our individual spirits are renewed, the Church experiences renewal and growth.

Beth and I are Roman Catholics who grew up and live in the United States, so I write from that perspective and for folks in that culture and environment. The lessons come from a mix of sources, insights my wife and others have shared plus my own experience, which includes over twenty-five years of teaching adults in the parish, ten years of leading Lenten missions, and over forty years working in the Catholic Charismatic Renewal. The Holy Spirit has taught me in many ways and blessed me through many excellent teachers, other Christians I have worked with and members of the communities where I have been a part. As we go forward, wherever possible I will provide illustrations from my own experience as well as references to help deepen understanding.

We begin our journey with a look at the goal of spiritual growth and maturity. What is this "narrow gate" Jesus tells us to strive for? After all, if we don't have a clear vision of where we are going, it will be difficult to make the correct decisions to get us there. The ultimate goal is obvious—to inherit eternal life, i.e., to "be saved"—

*Introduction*

but what goals should we seek to achieve in this life? How is the narrow gate, and the road beyond, marked? How can we know we are on that narrow, constricted path? If we compare the Scripture above with other verses about salvation, we discover that the answer may not always be so obvious. Certainly it would be sad to come to the right gate and then just pass it by because we didn't recognize it for what it is.

# Chapter One

## The Narrow Gate

*As he was setting out on a journey, a man ran up, knelt down before him, and asked him, "Good teacher, what must I do to inherit eternal life?" Jesus answered him, "Why do you call me good? No one is good but God alone. You know the commandments: You shall not kill; you shall not commit adultery; you shall not steal; you shall not bear false witness; you shall not defraud; honor your father and your mother.'" He replied and said to him, "Teacher, all of these I have observed from my youth." Jesus, looking at him, loved him and said to him, "You are lacking in one thing. Go, sell what you have, and give to [the] poor and you will have treasure in heaven; then come, follow me." At that statement his face fell, and he went away sad, for he had many possessions.*

*Jesus looked around and said to his disciples, "How hard it is for those who have wealth to enter the kingdom of God!" The disciples were amazed at his words. So Jesus again said to them in reply, "Children, how hard it is to enter the kingdom of God! It is easier for a camel to pass through [the] eye of [a] needle than for one who is rich to enter the kingdom of God." They were exceedingly astonished and said among themselves, "Then who can be saved?" Jesus looked at them and said, "For human beings it is impossible, but not for God. All things are possible for God." (Mark 10:17–27)*

Let's consider this passage from Mark 10:17–27 (see also Matt 19:16–26 and Luke 18:18–27) about the rich young man who asks, "Good teacher, what must I do to inherit eternal life?" Jesus' initial answer is, "You know the commandments…" When the young man replies, "All of these I have observed from my youth," Mark notes that Jesus "loved him" and calls him to take another step forward: "Go, sell what you have, and give to the poor, and you will have treasure in heaven." Then Jesus calls him to take yet another step: "Come, follow me." Jesus begins by establishing a point of common understanding with the young man (the commandments) and then draws him outward and onward by inviting him to remove the distractions (riches) from his life and follow him. Here Jesus is showing us the narrow door by drawing the young man into a personal relationship with himself (see *CCC*, 754, 787). Jesus is the door, but, as we shall see, the nature of relationship we are called to have with him is what makes the door narrow and explains why it can be difficult to find and enter.

The first difficulty we are likely to encounter is our perception of what it costs to enter into a proper relationship with Jesus. Like the rich young man, for almost all of us that first big step of removing distractions will seem too big to swallow all in one chunk, especially on the spur of the moment. Hopefully, a broader perspective can help ease the sticker shock. For starters, here are a few key points:

1. *Recognize that the rewards are great.* Like a football coach at the initial meeting before practice begins, Jesus is addressing a new member of his team. And, like many coaches, Jesus lays it on the line. Spiritual growth, just like sports or any worthwhile human endeavor, requires commitment, dedication, and focus. Jesus makes that clear. Fortunately, there are great rewards to be obtained in this life, not to mention in the next; spiritual growth is not a matter of all giving and no receiving. We grow and develop in the process and enjoy increased skills, a sense of accomplishment, meaningful relationships, and the game itself as we move forward, work hard, and stay with the program.

2. *Avoid the trap of making à priori assumptions.* Don't assume you will have to become a priest or nun, evangelize cannibals in some dark jungle, engage in public protest, or do whatever else seems repugnant to you. God's call is unique; it's tailor-

made for each of us. The more you experience his call for you, the more you will absolutely love it. Here is a paradox: what appears on the surface that seems to be "binding," a surrender of our freedom, is in reality very different. There is a tremendous sense of joy and freedom in being able to do what you were designed, trained, and gifted to do. Moreover, God has been working very hard to provide guidance to you all your life, so unless you've done nothing but pull against the bit all that time, you will probably find you are already pretty close to where God wants you in terms of your state in life, occupation, required skills, etc. Scripture speaks of "pruning," not transplanting. (Compare John 15:1-7 and Matthew 13:24-30.)

3. *Be patient if you find yourself in very difficult and unpleasant circumstances.* Jesus also said: "Come to me, all you who labor and are burdened, and I will give you rest. Take my yoke upon you and learn from me, for I am meek and humble of heart; and you will find rest for your selves. For my yoke is easy, and my burden light." (Matthew 11:28–30). Though it may be difficult to believe, Jesus is the great fixer and healer, so be patient and hang in there. Often we must endure a difficulty for some time (much longer than we would like) because he works gently and his solution tends to be both broader and deeper than the relief we are seeking. With time you will see that this very positive perspective is justified.

4. *Jesus loves you, just like he loved the rich young man, and wants the very best for you.* After all, "the heavens and the earth, the sea and all the rest of creation exist" for our benefit (*CCC*, 358). I have every confidence that the rich young man's story does not end where the Scripture leaves off. Jesus knows his business, and the Holy Spirit is continually at work. In the end, I suspect Jesus got his man.

5. *You only need to leave behind the distractions—that which hinders your spiritual growth or your work for the Lord.* The rest of the good things in the world and more are there for you to keep and enjoy, "good measure, packed together, shaken down and overflowing" (Luke 6:38). Just be aware that the process takes time and discernment.

## A Personal Relationship with Jesus

Now let's look at that next step, the narrow door itself: developing a "personal relationship" with Jesus. What does that really mean? Is there a standard to judge oneself against? Most Catholics can relate at least one, perhaps even a few, instances in their lives when they really *knew* the Lord was present, either speaking to them or helping them in some way. An example is the experience of a friend of mine. Traveling with a church group in a remote area of Arizona, the bus broke down out in the middle of nowhere. After assessing the situation, the group gathered together and prayed. Not long after, a single car came down the highway. The driver, a mechanic and the only person within 100 miles that *could* help them, stopped and fixed the problem. For my friend, this event became a lasting memory that led to a deep personal faith.

Single events like this are very valuable because they are the seeds from which a deep personal relationship grows—the starting point for growth, but they are not the final product. Unfortunately, too many of us are plodding along in our Christian walk with just a few of these faith seeds kept marginally alive, it seems, by the benefits of the Church and participating in the Liturgy. Any significant growth past that point is, or at least appears to be, missing. Scripture, Church teaching, and the witness of the saints all indicate we should experience a much deeper relationship with Christ. Fundamentally, for one person to have a relationship with another, one must have direct, continuing personal contact and knowledge of the other person. Relationship implies more than memories and knowledge about the other person; it implies some level of ongoing interaction.

To gain a sense of what that relationship really means, let's look at John 15:1–10, especially verse 5, "I am the vine, you are the branches." We enter life as branches, without roots, cut off from the vine by original sin, slowly withering and dying because we lack the life-giving sap (the Holy Spirit) that comes only from the vine (Christ). In this condition our tendency is to turn in on ourselves out of self-concern—to conserve, nourish, and enjoy what life we have before it slips away. However, by baptism and confirmation we are grafted onto the true, living vine. For this the vine has been wounded, cut open, and from the branch also, dead wood must be removed. The end of the branch is inserted into the cut in the vine and the wound is bound. If the graft is good, a small stream of life-giving sap will begin to flow from the vine to the branch, and slowly the graft heals. In time the healing can become so complete that vine and branch become, in a sense, indistinguishable. They appear as one plant, with the intersection between the two discernible only by careful inspection. The life-giving sap flows freely from vine to branch and much fruit is borne.

Here is another paradox. We normally think of the natural, created world as very separate and very different from the supernatural. With the vine and branch, however, Christ tells us they have become so intermingled as to become inseparable. When Christ became man he took on a fully human nature so we can graft onto him; the branch and the vine are sufficiently the same. The branch never becomes the vine, but it shares the same divine life with the vine. This unity is deep and profound. The *Catechism of the Catholic Church* states it this way: "[God] gave himself to us through his Spirit. By the participation of the Spirit, we become communicants in the divine nature.... For this reason, those in whom the Spirit dwells are divinized" (*CCC*, 1988). Likewise: "For this is why the Word became man, and the Son of God became Son of Man: so that man, by entering into communion with the Word and thus receiving divine sonship, might become a son of God" (*CCC*, 460, quoting St. Irenaeus). Note the reference to communion in both quotations. Is it any surprise that *communion* with the divine nature involves *communication*—or at least our direct, personal understanding that our unity with the divine nature indeed exists?

This communion with the divine is exactly what we are looking for: to become inseparable from Christ so that when death occurs we end up with him and not cut off. In fact, St. Paul in his letter to the Ephesians says the Holy Spirit is the pledge, or first payment, of what it will be like in heaven, "… the first installment of our inheritance toward redemption as God's possession, to the praise of his glory." (Ephesians 1:14) The Trinity consists of three persons linked in perfect unity, communication, and love. By the Holy Spirit dwelling within us, God is working to draw each of us to himself, to that identical relationship of unity, communication, and love. This is the narrow door we need to strive to enter. Our entry is not complete until the next life, but it begins now.

While we might be able to grasp this concise but theological description of our goal, for most of us it's a goal that seems a million miles from our typical, very busy, secular lives. Well, take heart; it is not quite so far as one would think. Let's turn to the practical and put our focus on the long, often slow growth process that began at baptism. How are we to recognize that our being grafted onto the true Vine is working at all?

1. Consider the paradox we have just described. Human nature is designed and built for close unity and communication with God. Thus, the action of the Spirit does not *feel* supernatural or spectacular. Instead, usually it feels normal and natural.
2. Because it's so normal, we need to watch for it. There is a gift and skill involved in recognizing the shepherd's voice that will be covered in the following chapters, but for starters we

must cultivate the habit of taking reflective moments to think about what is happening in our lives.

3. There is a simplicity and goodness to the work of the Spirit. Think about someone handing you a pencil just when you need it—just when you realize the need but before you say anything. There's no question of the pencil's reality; it's in your hand. We should experience God watching over us just like that. Most often with the Lord, it is an idea or understanding that he hands you. The issue is recognizing that it is the Lord at work.

4. There are some prerequisites. Primarily, we must want God to be active in our life, and we must be willing to be transformed and led by him.

The spiritual life is a growth and learning process, so perhaps an example or two might be helpful here. These come from a time when God seemed to be working hard to help me understand; at least he was making his presence obvious for me. I think God prefers to whisper, but he will shout if we need it. One example comes from my own life; it happened one day while I was working at NASA. We were building a pallet of experiment hardware for a flight test on a tight schedule. I had three errands to run at different places: parts to pick up, papers to have signed, that sort of thing. I'll call them A, B, and C—that's the order I planned to do them as I rushed out the door. On my way out I had a sense that I should change the order to C, A, B. I promptly ignored that little nudge and proceeded with my original plan, only to find the person I needed to see at stop A had just left, the B office was closed, and C was on a short errand of his own. In the end, I accomplished my mission, but it took most of the afternoon rather than the hour I had hoped. That afternoon was part of the long process that taught me two key lessons:

1. God is interested in our daily work and will help us with it.

2. It takes training to hear and correctly respond to God's voice.

A second example sticks out in my memory because my level of desperation was deeper and because it was also a confirmation of a ministry we were involved with at the time. I had decided to make seven wooden signs, one each for the families that would be joining in a new endeavor at a Monday evening event at our church. I'm a fairly accomplished woodworker, and I had seen similar signs made at a craft fair. I thought it would be a piece of cake: cut the redwood boards to length, rout out the letters with a router, spray with a can of paint to fill in the letters, and sand off the paint on the surface of the board so the letters would show clearly. Saturday morning I bought the redwood, drove home, and began laying out the project. I only had Saturday and Sunday afternoon to do the job.

Panic #1: I realized I needed three more feet of redwood than I figured when I bought it, and the only lumberyard that carries it closed at noon. But then, I measured the boards and found that I had three more feet of board than I paid for! I guess the guy at the yard didn't want to take the trouble to cut it. What a blessing!

The work proceeded: mark, cut, rout, spray the lettering with paint, let it dry. It was now Sunday afternoon. I took my belt sander with its new belt and began sanding off the excess paint. Ten seconds later the belt was plugged with paint and very little had been removed. Clearly the spray paint I had used was very different from whatever the guy at the craft fair had used; he had sanded it off immediately without any problem. I sat on a stool in my shop, eyes closed – praying. *Lord, what do I do now?*

I opened my eyes and immediately saw the red handle of a draw knife protruding slightly from the corner of a shelf. I had bought the knife on a whim some years before and never found a use for it (and have not found many since, either). It was the perfect tool to shave off the paint! The rest was quick and easy. These signs were greatly appreciated. The memory has been lasting for me.

## A Transformed Perspective

Your perspective on God and religion becomes very different because of days like the ones I've just described when you recognize his presence at work in your daily life. It is not the single events—those can always be explained away—but rather the way those events fit into a consistent pattern of life that makes the difference. Simplicity, goodness, and truth become evident to your spirit. Life becomes a joint venture: you and the Holy Spirit, you and Jesus, you and the Father. That knowledge, along with the peace, faith, and other fruit it brings is all the gift of the Holy Spirit. The noted Catholic theologian of the last century, Hans Urs von Balthasar, in his excellent book *Prayer* points out the strong identification of the Holy Spirit with Truth in John's gospel, and how that truth creates conviction in the human heart. Regarding the fruits of the Spirit, he says, "It is impossible to say what comes from man and what from God."[2] We begin to realize that the natural and divine are inseparable. This perspective is in opposition to secular culture with its emphasis on physical reality and reliance on science, but it fits very well with a human nature formed "in the image and likeness" of the Creator. Some feel that such a direct experience of God would be "spooky," but in fact the opposite is true. Experiencing God is an expression of his peace and love, and it feels that way.

How is this direct person-to-person relationship with Jesus to be found? Well, we must seek it, but, in reality, it can't be found; it has to find you. However, God is eager to deepen his relationship with us; it is a key work of the Holy Spirit. (See Luke 11:9–13.) He comes to each of us individually, at the time and place that is best for us and for his plan. It also depends on us; are we ready? Are we seeking? Are we doing our part?

---

[2] **Prayer,** by Hans Urs von Balthasar, English translation by Graham Harrison, Ignatius Press, 1986, p 78

Jesus gave us the starting point in the tale of the rich young man, where we began this chapter. Are we avoiding sin and distractions? Maybe you are doing that but still have no sense that God is directly communicating with you. The truth is that God is already communicating with you extensively, but you do not yet realize it. For example, what about your conscience? The *Catechism* says, "When he listens to his conscience, the prudent man can hear God speaking" (*CCC*, 1777). Or what about your perception when you are staring at a computer printout, trying to solve a problem, or walking into a room full of people? How often do you see or hear just what you need to see or hear? What about those good ideas that just seem to pop into your head at times when you are thinking about something completely different? Are these the result of some hidden process in the human brain, or is the Holy Spirit nudging us? Try asking God to reveal when he is speaking to you, and watch what happens.

Here, then, is the narrow gate we seek to enter. I must note, it is clearly narrow with obstacles to either side. On the one hand, the relationship must be experiential; otherwise it is not personal. However, look at the examples I have given; the experiences are very subtle, natural–seeming perceptions that God is guiding, protecting, affirming, or loving a person. The "experience" is really a conviction deep within the heart brought about by the Holy Spirit. It is knowing the voice of the divine shepherd (John 10:4), connected or not to some physical event. It is dangerous to seek spiritual experiences themselves, especially "spiritual highs" which can and do occur on occasion. This would be, in reality, seeking a self-gratification that only leads to endless searching; it bears little good fruit. Rather, we must seek the Shepherd himself. On the other hand, we must not deny the importance of the experiential dimension; this can lead to knowing about God in an academic sense without knowing God in person or to obeying God's law but not obeying God himself.

To summarize, the objective of our spiritual journey is the transformation of our life so that we live in deep unity with God, a

*The Narrow Gate*

very personal and direct relationship brought about through the work of the Holy Spirit. There is bound to be an ebb and flow in the intensity of our union with the Lord as the times and seasons of our lives change. In his parables, Jesus often used the relationship between a king or land-owner who temporarily leaves, later to return, as an example of the relationship between God and his servants. However, the relationship remains independent of where the master seems to be. Both our experience and Church teaching indicate that a continual, ongoing relationship with the Lord—a loving relationship we live and experience—is a practical and useful benchmark. As we proceed, the nature of this relationship will become clearer. Next we'll turn our attention to understanding the process that will help get us there. Have confidence; it's easier than you think.

**For Further Reflection:**

- Luke 11:9-13 — God is eager to send the Holy Spirit to his people.
- Psalm 127:1-2 — In all aspects of life, without God there is no progress.
- Exodus 19 and 25:8 — Even in the Old Testament, God shows that he considers his people as special and wishes to dwell with them.

## Chapter Two

# <u>A Vision of the Kingdom</u>

> *In a large household there are vessels not only of gold and silver but also of wood and clay, some for lofty and others for humble use. If anyone cleanses himself of these things, he will be a vessel for lofty use, dedicated, beneficial to the master of the house, ready for every good work. So turn from youthful desires and pursue righteousness, faith, love, and peace, along with those who call on the Lord with purity of heart. (2 Timothy 2:20–22)*

Now that the goal of spiritual growth—a daily, personal unity with Jesus—has been clearly identified, we can begin to develop the picture of how to get there or, more accurately, how we can do our part to cooperate with God's grace in order to grow quickly. We begin with a general description of the process. Again, this will be developed by looking at the central thrust of Jesus' teaching. The premise is simple: when our focus is the same as Christ's teaching, the narrow road (i.e., what we need in order to come into unity with him) becomes clear. At first the answers may seem a little on the mundane side—a few ordinary-looking stones in the field of Christian teaching—but, as the details become clearer in the following chapters, the pearls will show forth.

Let's begin by painting the picture with a few key Scriptures:

### Kingdom

> *From that time on, Jesus began to preach and say, "Repent, for the kingdom of heaven is at hand" (Matthew 4:17).*

## A Vision of the Kingdom

Matthew tells us that the focus of Jesus' teaching was the establishment of the kingdom of God. The idea of a kingdom is likely to be a bit foreign to us, since many modern governments, including our own, are based on the ideals of democracy. We tend to equate kingdom with "nation" or "state" and miss the point. The Israelites in biblical times actually had a king, a person selected and anointed by God to speak for God and lead the people. The king set the policy and made the key decisions. The people of the kingdom were required to support and obey the king. The king's word, by divine right, was law. In a kingdom, power and authority emanate from the king, not from the people. As our picture comes into focus we will see that, in the New Testament world, Jesus is the King, and his orders are communicated to us by the Holy Spirit (see Romans 14:9 and John 14:26).

### Inspiration by the Holy Spirit

> *...I did not speak on my own, but the Father who sent me commanded me what to say and speak. And I know that his commandment is eternal life. So what I say, I say as the Father told me. (John 12:49–50; see also Deuteronomy 18:18; John 5:19; John 14:10).*

These Scriptures make it clear that Jesus was not operating on his own; rather, everything he did was in unity and in obedience with the Father. There must have been close communication between Jesus and the Father because this type of unity demands it. Thus, since we are called to imitate Jesus, we too are invited to similar close communication and deep unity with him. The Holy Spirit has been sent to develop this deep union with us.

Here we encounter a significant obstacle that must be avoided. Secular culture creates a strong tendency for us to interpret the above passages in only a general sense—i.e., the Holy Spirit provides only a general understanding of the faith, morals, and God's plan of salvation. This is simply not true, as a little prayer and contemplation of the unity of the Godhead will soon make clear. Far beyond the general, the instruction of the Holy Spirit can be very specific with respect to times and situations and also very personal. It is still correct that the general understanding is also a gift of the Holy Spirit. In that case the gift carries with it a clear sense of what is truth. This is a key point in the Gospel of John, chapters 14 through 17. Note in particular John 16:13–15:

> *But when he comes, the Spirit of truth, he will guide you to all truth. He will not speak on his own, but he will speak what he hears, and will declare to you the things that are coming. He will glorify me, because he will take from what is mine and declare it to you. Everything that the Father has is mine; for this reason I told you that he will take from what is mine and declare it to you.*
>
> *Also, John 17:25-26: Righteous Father, the world also does not know you, but I know you, and they know that you sent me. I made known to them your name and I will make it known, that the love with which you loved me may be in them and I in them.*

## Servanthood

> *Who, then, is the faithful and prudent servant, whom his master has put in charge of his household to distribute to them their food at the proper time? Blessed is that servant whom his master on his arrival finds doing so. Amen, I say to you, he will put him in charge of all his property. (Matthew 24:45-47; see also Matthew 25:14–30; Luke 12:42–48; Luke 17:7–10; Matt 21:28–32 and 21:33-46; Mark 12:1–12; Luke 20:9–19; Mark 13,34–37; Luke 12:36–38).*

The relationship between a servant and his master, which includes related topics such as faithfulness to duty, watchfulness, and stewardship, is one of the major themes of Jesus' teaching. In fact, it is the single most dominant topic of his parables. Reviewing a list of thirty-five "major parables" in the back of my old (1957 vintage) Confraternity Bible, I found that fifteen (43 percent) addressed servanthood topics; the kingdom of God came in second with twelve parables (34 percent).

In particular, there is emphasis on the need for a servant to be faithful to the charge given him by his master, especially when the master is away. Jesus is clearly setting a standard for Christian behavior, and he does not mince words. Consider the final words of Luke 17:7–10:

> *Who among you would say to your servant who has just come in from plowing or tending sheep in the field, "Come here immediately and take your place at table"? Would he not rather say to him, "Prepare something for me to eat. Put on your apron and wait on me while I eat and drink. You may eat and drink when I am finished"? Is he grateful to that servant because he did what was commanded? So should it be with you. When you have done all you have been commanded, say, "We are unprofitable servants; we have done what we were obliged to do."*

## Vine and Branches

> I am the vine, and you are the branches. *(John 15:5; see also verses 1–4; 6–10).*

This well-known passage expresses essentially the same truth as the passages discussed above but from a very different angle. Jesus is the vine; we are the branches. The branches must remain attached to the vine in order to bear fruit, and fruit is essential both to building the kingdom and building personal faith. The complete and gentle unity between the vine and branches, the common sap running through both, is a much more appealing image than Jesus as master and we as servants or, as some Scripture translations express it, as slaves. The latter image grates against our human ego that drives us so strongly to want our own way, to be our own boss. However, both images express the same reality. When it is *love* that binds us to the master and it is our free choice to dwell in that bond/bondage, then the struggle disappears. The reality that remains is unity of heart and purpose, and that "sap" is the grace of the Holy Spirit that flows freely from the vine to the branches.

*A Vision of the Kingdom*

Pulling these various images together, this is the picture we find: just as the character of the Godhead, the Trinity, is complete and total unity, complete and total love, complete singleness of purpose and will among the three persons, so we are called to a relationship with God that is essentially identical to that within the Trinity. The roles differ, certainly, but the nature of the relationship mirrors that of the Godhead itself. God is God: Creator of the universe, Source of all life and truth, Lord and Master, Savior and Sanctifier. We are human creatures, weak in flesh and spirit, servants and slaves, implementers of the Lord's purpose, and doers of his word. But our relationship with God, if we choose to accept it, is unity, love, and singleness of purpose, within the roles he has set for each of us. That is what it means to be his friends (see John 15:15) and adopted children of God (see Romans 8:15; Galatians 4:5; Ephesians 1:5). Once you understand this, once the picture pops into focus, it seems like the whole of Scripture shouts the same message in confirmation—from the Old Testament covenant of Moses where God comes to dwell with his people (see Exodus 19:5–6 and 29:43–46) to the poignant passages of the New (especially John's Gospel) where Jesus establishes the new covenant in his blood and in power, sending the Holy Spirit upon his followers at Pentecost.

Church teaching in this area is found in the *Catechism of the Catholic Church*, paragraphs 1988 through 2003. Paragraph 1988 begins with allusion to the vine and branches and quotes St. Athanasius: "….we become communicants in the divine nature… For this reason, those in whom the Spirit dwells are divinized." These passages cover the works of the Spirit, justification and grace, with paragraph 2003 emphasizing how grace enables us to collaborate in God's work of salvation and building up the Church (i.e., the kingdom).

It might also help to look at some other well-established ideas that support these concepts. For example, consider the general scope and message of Scripture: in establishing the kingdom, God strongly desires to work out his plan of salvation through us, his people. St.

Teresa of Avila said, "Christ has no body now but yours. No hands, no feet on earth but yours." Beginning several thousand years before the birth of Jesus, God started with Abraham and his family, followed by Moses, the judges and prophets, and David and the kings of Judah and Israel, on down to the Virgin Mary, the apostles and the Church Fathers. Throughout the ages, God slowly revealed himself, his plan, and his way of life. And the response and role of people throughout history, named and unnamed, was crucial to what has been accomplished and is still being accomplished—creation of a Godly culture, writing and preserving the Bible, a lasting and close relationship with God through the Church.

The New Testament makes it very clear that this work is to continue in each of us (see Mark 16:14–18; Acts 2:17–18, John 20:22–23; 21:15–17). It is extremely important to note that the work we are called to often includes spiritual works: forgiveness, healing, prophesying, seeing visions, and evangelizing—all of the charismatic gifts of the Spirit (see 1 Corinthians 12). Since these works are clearly beyond mere human capability, the need for close unity with God becomes obvious. The antithesis of this point also gives food for serious thought: how much of God's will is not being accomplished because too few are willing to step up and act on God's behalf?

Returning to the biblical concept of servant, a useful illustration can be found in the movie *Ben-Hur,* starring Charlton Heston.[3] An excellent movie for many reasons, it won eleven Academy Awards in 1959. In this film the relationships in the household of Judah Ben-Hur, our hero, and his family, servants, and slaves, illustrate an ideal concept of servanthood. Over the long years of exile and struggle between the Prince of Hur and the powers of Rome, the household maintains a powerful, sacrificial love for and faithfulness to the master, and vice versa. This is the relationship Jesus calls us to, illustrated in his many parables. The relationship is clearly master–servant, but it is a relationship built and bound together in love,

---

[3] *Ben-Hur, William Wyler, director; Metro-Golden-Mayer, 1959.*

faithfulness, and mutual respect. Here authority relationships are in right order, and individual initiative and dignity are preserved and encouraged. God calls each of us to enter into this type of relationship with him. Indeed, he relies on us to enter and embrace this relationship of master and servant so we can implement our portion of his saving work.

In today's culture, there isn't much glory or prestige associated with being a servant, but consider how important service is to our lives. Something as common as dinner out at a restaurant can become either a pleasant memory or an exasperating experience, depending on the service of the waiter. I still recall two such dinners that took place over forty years ago, both in very "nice" restaurants. The first was in San Francisco. The service was incredibly excellent, completely unobtrusive but so responsive it seemed that the waiter was reading our minds. I no sooner thought, *I would like some more tea*, than he was at my elbow with tea in hand. The opposite was the case one night in Las Vegas, where our *team* of waiters spent the entire time laughing and talking by the kitchen door. We couldn't get their attention and almost ended up late for out next appointment. We left them a very small tip, wanting them to know that we had not neglected them. The difference between these two dining experiences was not a lack of technical skill; it was the attention and focus on the customer and serving with a heart for the job. This is what God desires from us—service with focus and attention to his will and a heart for the work. And when it is God's work, he adds grace so that it can lead to much more than pleasant memories: it changes lives.

Secular culture struggles against the role of servant in another way: it tries to create a fear that serving others means we would be losing our freedom. Freedom, after all, is one of the great American ideals. Nobody wants to go through life with somebody else always telling them what to do. That is as it should be. The fear that arises here is the result of little distortions; the truth is much more sanguine. First, freedom is always limited; this is necessary to make society work.

Second, God always honors our free will. Third, and here is the significant point, God is not just "somebody else"; he is the One who created us, keeps us alive, provides for our needs, and loves us abundantly. He knows us better than we know ourselves, and he knows the future and understands each situation we face.

It is important to note that God only gives guidance when it is necessary for his plan or our welfare or someone else's—otherwise he leaves the decisions for us to make. True, we are accepting some limitations on our options, but in reality all we are giving up is our freedom to make harmful or inconsequential independent choices in exchange for being on a team that does significant, beautiful, exciting work of lasting benefit. I like to think of freedom's limitations like a railroad locomotive; in a sense it is "stuck," destined to remain on its track. If only it were free of the track it could move freely in any direction—but not very far and not very productively. However, on the track it can travel both far and fast, pulling trains across the countryside, the breeze flowing past its windows, doing what it was meant to do.

**Key Takeaways**

- God is establishing his kingdom in the world *now*, among us today. Certainly the kingdom extends into heaven, but this life on earth is where spiritual growth must occur.

- Our role in this kingdom is to be God's servants. The many servant parables make it clear that servanthood is a priority. It is also a role that can expand if we are good and faithful. We may become stewards, ambassadors, and friends of Christ, but our basic role is always that of a servant.

- Taking Jesus as our model, being an effective servant means living and working in close unity with the Father, Son, and Holy Spirit. Good fruit only comes from the one true Vine,

*A Vision of the Kingdom*

so our action must spring primarily from the promptings of the Spirit. Here discernment of God's guidance is very important. We are expected to step forward of our own initiative, but in harmony with God's will.

Now, given this picture, how does this understanding help our spiritual growth? What must we do? The answer is both simple and crucial: *For spiritual growth to occur, we must commit to this vision of the Kingdom and our place within it, just as Jesus explained it.* Truly, there are many ways to support our growth as Christians:

- Experience yields wisdom

- Study yields the understanding of Scripture and Church teaching

- Self-discipline yields self–control

- Love of neighbor and service to the community help increase our sense of compassion and justice

All our efforts for God bear fruit. But growing deeper spiritually requires our total acceptance of our identity as God servants. This acceptance establishes a correct relationship with God, and this is our foundation. God is God; we are his creatures, his servants. This foundation also sets the correct perspective for each decision we make. Our purpose, our intent, is always to further the kingdom; God's plan is now "ours." Spiritual growth means growth in unity with God, and that must always be on his terms.

**For Further Reflection**

- Romans 14:9, John 14:26 — Jesus is Lord of the living, and the Holy Spirit communicates his instructions.

- Mark 16:14-18 — God calls us to take part in his work of salvation.
- John 20:22-23; 21:15-17 — The Holy Spirit directs the apostles to do spiritual works.
- Acts 2:17-18 — The Spirit will enable *all* God's people to perform spiritual works, such as prophesy.
- CCC #1988-2003 — Discussion of how the Holy Spirit transforms our relationship with God.

## Chapter Three

## Service, the Kingdom, and the Cross

*Whoever loves father or mother more than me is not worthy of me, and whoever loves son or daughter more than me is not worthy of me; and whoever does not take up his cross and follow after me is not worthy of me. Whoever finds his life will lose it, and whoever loses his life for my sake will find it. (Matthew 10:37–39).*

So far we have established several principles of spiritual growth:

1. Our goal is to grow into a direct, personal relationship with Jesus, and this is implemented by the Holy Spirit.

2. It's important to understand God's vision for his kingdom here on earth and that all of us are called to participate.

3. Crucial to participation in the kingdom is our acceptance of our role as servants of God. We noted the high priority Jesus placed on the servant's role in his teaching.

4. Focusing on servanthood, we recognize the increasing necessity for unity with the Trinity. Thus we must "grow in Christ" as a means to gain experience, wisdom, and holiness.

5. Just appearing on the horizon, we begin to see how our servant role will include spiritual works. The path will lead to more than "serve one another" in the natural sense although our natural human service is never left behind.

### Service Comes First

We now turn to some important aspects of Catholic practice and teaching that will help in the growth process. You should not find any great surprises here, but you will note some shifts in priority and increased emphasis on subtle points about well-established concepts. To simply illustrate what I mean, the old *Baltimore Catechism*'s answer to the question of why God made us is "to know Him, to love Him, and to serve Him in this world, and to be happy with him for ever in heaven."[4] The sequence implied here is certainly correct for children, but for more mature Christians seeking spiritual growth, the order should be switched. Service—working with God to accomplish his purpose—becomes our entry or starting point. This, in turn, results in a deeper knowledge, appreciation of his work, and a more profound love.

In the previous chapter we focused on the parables as the means to define principles that form the focus of Jesus' teaching. Since his sacrifice on the cross is the acknowledged centerpiece of Jesus' saving mission, one might argue that, if we really want to be confident we have found the focus of His teaching, we should also look there. Certainly any teaching on the conditions of discipleship and spiritual growth should include reflection on Scriptures such as Matthew 10:37–39, which began this chapter; Matthew 11:28–30; Mark 8:34–35; Luke 14:26–27; and Luke 9:23-24. These Scriptures make it clear that we, as followers of Christ, must be willing to carry our own crosses in union and imitation of Jesus. His mission was to open a path to salvation for all mankind, and the pivotal point in accomplishing that was his death on the cross, followed by his resurrection. Jesus calls us to take part in his work of salvation and not fail at the crucial points of our mission—i.e. our crosses.

## The Doctrine of the Cross

It concerns me that the full scope and importance of the doctrine of the cross is not fully appreciated by many Catholics. Perhaps it has just been my personal experience, but commentary on these

---

[4] Baltimore Catechism (Charlotte, NC: St. Benedict Press, Tan Books, 2010) p.7.

Scriptures always seems to be narrowly focused on one key aspect of the doctrine to the detriment of the broader implications. The typical logic runs something like this: "Jesus conquered sin and death by his passion and death on the cross." *Guilty pleasure* (illicit sex, pornography, excessive drinking or drug use, etc., you know the list) is one class of sins that Jesus conquered by his acceptance of the exact opposite— innocent suffering. An important application to our lives comes when we are suffering; Jesus allows us to offer up our sufferings and join them to his. In this way our suffering also contributes to the remission of sin and redemption. While Jesus' sacrifice was both complete and sufficient, it is also "open" so that more can be contributed, and that is how we are invited to participate in it. By this means, our suffering has great value and benefit.

This understanding is a considerable consolation to those who are suffering. It is a great gift from the Lord. Unfortunately it seems to be popular to emphasize this point at the expense of other aspects of the cross; a person can easily get the idea that the doctrine ends there. One detrimental side effect is that suffering tends to be too easily accepted, even idealized, while an appreciation of Jesus the Healer is correspondingly undervalued.

There are two other major classes of sin besides guilty pleasure, and these are related to *sins of omission*—things we should do but don't. Specifically, they are *disobedience to God* and *lack of faith in God*. As with guilty pleasure, Jesus, by his action on the cross, also conquers these. Jesus is the perfect example both of obedience to the Father and trust in him. Recall Matthew 26:39:

> *He advanced a little and fell prostrate in prayer, saying, "My Father, if it is possible, let this cup pass from me; yet, not as I will, but as you will."*

Based on his understanding of spiritual reality and his Father's wishes, Jesus acts against every human and worldly instinct to accomplish the mission his Father entrusted to him, the redemption of mankind. Herein lies the great challenge of Christianity and of discipleship: to live in obedience to God's will, trusting his provision even in times when human judgment, science, and worldly wisdom all shout, "Go another way."

## Deep Obedience and Faith

Of course, the importance of obedience and faith is not exactly a secret within Christian circles. What I'm trying to get at is an understanding of the depth and magnitude of that obedience and faith which the Lord holds out as our goal. Take the time I was waterskiing on Lake Tahoe, a lake famous for its great depth and clarity. I had learned to waterski on Wisconsin's Green Bay, a body of water that certainly lived up to its name, especially in those days. (It has since gained much clarity.) But it was truly a shock heading out over Tahoe and looking down. I could clearly see the rocks forty or more feet below me, but it seemed like a hundred. I had lived for years within an hour's drive of Lake Tahoe, but suddenly, "deep and clear" took on a whole new meaning.

Similarly, there is what we might call a "level one" understanding of this challenge, where obedience is equated with avoidance of sin and faith means living a nominal Christian lifestyle—attending church regularly and acting with love and respect for one another. This is the basic understanding of Christianity, and certainly it poses a significant challenge to all of us as we try to meet this mark. However, when one looks at the strongly worded demands of these Scriptures describing the doctrine of the cross in terms of faith and obedience, coupled with others on discipleship, a much deeper understanding begins to emerge. And again we have an amazing paradox: while one would expect a deeper call to faith and obedience to be more difficult to live, in fact, it is *not*. It is both easier and more fruitful because it is a closer walk with Jesus. Spiritual power (sanctifying grace) enables us to gain many blessings and avoid much suffering, especially the heart-stabbing suffering associated with sin. This path also provides a sense of meaning and accomplishment because God uses us to provide significant blessings to others.

The cross was integral to Jesus' mission; it was the work he became man to accomplish, and through it, he opened the path for our salvation. Therefore, Jesus calls each of his disciples—each of us—to carry our cross in imitation of him. This is best understood as a call to carry out our own mission as God's servants; we might say that "cross" equals "mission," or perhaps "service," "responsibility," or "burden."

We also can equate "cross" with "suffering" because of the idea of redemptive suffering described above—but this should not be the *only* association made. If it is, one runs into a number of scriptural as well as pragmatic problems. For example, Luke 9:23–24 says we should pick up our cross "daily." Does this mean we should inflict some form of suffering upon ourselves each day? Few would interpret it that way. It also does not square well with the concept of a God who loves us. It certainly seems to run into conflict with Scriptures like Matthew 11:28–30:

> *Come to me, all you who labor and are burdened, and I will give you rest. Take my yoke upon you and learn from me, for I am meek and humble of heart; and you will find rest for yourselves. For my yoke is easy, and my burden light.*

Realizing that each of us has a place in God's kingdom, a membership in God's household, the interpretation that each day we are called to fulfill the responsibilities and duties of that membership provides a more direct and simpler understanding. To be clear, associating the cross primarily with mission still includes some expectation of suffering. Scripture specifically mentions persecution, for example. It also includes self-discipline, hard work, placing our trust in God, and all the other demands of discipleship.

## The Importance of Discipleship

To move us forward on the path to spiritual growth, a key lesson of the cross is the tremendous importance God places on discipleship—that is, on our service and participation in his plan. After all, when one looks at the whole of salvation history, in both the Old and New Testaments, one sees that God's people are always involved in a way that is integral to God's work of salvation. Consider the role of the Patriarchs, the Judges, the Kings, and the Prophets in the Old Testament. Think of all those unnamed people who wrote, edited, and preserved Scripture. In the New Testament, we can observe Mary, the apostles and disciples, likewise, the steady witness and leadership of the saints and Church which continues in our own time. While God is always the prime mover, he always works in conjunction with his people. As individuals, we might not make the annals of Church history, but together we form the core of the faith and the strength of the Church. Man is a very social creature and our cultures are very important to how we act. We may not be conscious of it, but the small things we do that show faithfulness to God impact our culture in a way that makes it easier for others to follow the truth.

The point is that God is performing a great work, and he wants us to be part of it! To return to a sports analogy, God is building a team and sending it out on the playing field of life. He wants each of us to be effective members of that team, and that requires dedication. Some may call it "sacrifice," but I don't believe that term is quite accurate because that implies loss without any compensating gain. Such is not the case here. When you join a pro-football team, hoping to go to the Super Bowl, you know that dedication and "sacrifice" are required, but the gain is well worth the effort. Jesus went to the cross, knowing the price was worth it. Likewise, for each of us, the benefits are well worth the price, here in this lifetime as well as in the kingdom to come.

*Service, the Kingdom, and the Cross*

One key benefit is that our faith blunts the sharp point of suffering. While a certain amount of struggle and suffering comes to each of us, we know and experience that "all things work for good for those who love God." (Romans 8:28) Thus the sharp point that pierces the heart and oppresses the human spirit is deflected. For the Christian, there is always a path that enables us to emerge stronger and victorious from the experience. One of my friends lived very much in the "fast-lane" of local politics until the day he ended up in a wheelchair for the rest of his life. Later he always said it was the best thing that ever happened to him because of the spiritual blessings and peace that he experienced as a result.

My own experience has led me to realize that God will give us all good things *as long as they are good for us and do not stand in the way of the mission God has for us to do.* God's work always has priority, but God loves us greatly and is anxious to give us any blessing that will not harm us or distract us from his purposes. To understand this, we need to realize that it is always God, not us, that does the picking and choosing. Let me give an example that will show how I came to this conclusion. When I was young I loved folk music (and I still do). Good folk music has a way of expressing truth with beauty in a way that just draws my heart. If I had had any musical talent at all, I most certainly would have tried folk music rather than physics as a career. However, by God's providence, I had essentially no musical talent and could not even carry a simple tune, even though many in my family were very talented musically. In fact, one of my brothers did become a professional musician. Looking back now and understanding my personal weaknesses, I shudder to think where that path would have led me. A fruitful career in music takes more than musical talent; other gifts of character and intellect are needed that I lacked. Physics, on the other hand, led to a rewarding, interesting, and beneficial career. Psalm 16:6 says, "Pleasant places were measured out for me; fair to me indeed is my inheritance." Amen to that!

**Key Takeaways**

- Along with the teachings of Jesus, the cross itself, the very mission of Jesus, leads to the conclusion that the most important thing people can do is serve God.

- Our service is not meant to be limited to natural service; it also includes responsiveness to the Holy Spirit in a way that enables his spiritual gifts and graces to flow forth—especially through obedience and trust in the Father, as Christ taught us by his example.

- While service requires great commitment, dedication, and "sacrifice," it also allows us to share abundantly in the blessings of God's household.

- God generously gives us every blessing that does not stand in the way of his work and calling.

**For Further Reflection:**

- CCC #306–308 — Mankind is involved in God's creation and plan.
- Luke 15:11–32 — In the parable of the Prodigal Son, note the struggle of the elder brother because he fails to accept the full authority and blessing of his place in the household.

# Chapter Four

# Sin and the Sacraments

*Jesus said to them, "I am the bread of life; whoever comes to me will never hunger, and whoever believes in me will never thirst. But I told you that although you have seen [me], you do not believe. Everything that the Father gives me will come to me, and I will not reject anyone who comes to me, because I came down from heaven not to do my own will but the will of the one who sent me. And this is the will of the one who sent me, that I should not lose anything of what he gave me, but that I should raise it [on] the last day. For this is the will of my Father, that everyone who sees the Son and believes in him may have eternal life, and I shall raise him [on] the last day" (John 6:35–40).*

We have been dealing with key concepts of spiritual growth that can, unfortunately, appear so ethereal and lofty that they seem impossible to grasp and master in a tangible way. Concepts help us understand the "what" and the "why"—but not the "how." Hopefully the previous chapters made the goals and objectives of spiritual growth clearer to you, but now what? From here on we turn to the very practical steps and processes needed to make spiritual growth a reality. We start with a look at sin and its best antidote, the sacraments.

**Sins and Sinfulness**

You are probably thinking, "Yes, of course I need to overcome my sinfulness in order to grow spiritually." Wrong! If there are *sins* you have already committed, by all means repent and make use of the sacrament of penance as soon as you can. But *sinfulness*, that weakness you are probably very aware of, that knowledge that you will more than likely be sinning again in the not too distant future—this is another matter. *The road to spiritual growth is for sinful people.* While it is definitely true that sinfulness and godliness are not compatible, we need to be very clear that a major benefit of working on spiritual growth is that it helps remedy our sinfulness. The positive drives out the negative. Moreover, the effectiveness of willpower is highly overrated.

There is more to sin than meets the eye—not only more problems from sinning, but more blessings from avoiding it. For example, I remember one Saturday afternoon several years ago. At the time, I was considering retirement from my day job in aerospace. I was starting to feel my age, and I was concerned about some potential health issues (that, thankfully, never materialized). As a result, I had been struggling for several weeks to fight off a mild depression and keep a healthy, positive attitude. This particular Saturday I went to confession, as I always try to do on a regular basis. I don't recall what was on my "list" that afternoon (and I wouldn't tell you if I did), but I clearly recall the priest explaining that they were venial sins. About an hour later, I suddenly realized the sense of depression and concern about my health was gone. I mean undeniably gone, and it did not return. I felt great! Then I realized what was going on: those "mere venial" sins had left me open to attack from the Evil One.

## Not So Small After All

This incident helped me realize that what we consider "small" sins are, in reality, more serious than we might otherwise think, especially in terms of the suffering they cause. People generally believe in justice, i.e., for each transgression there should be some consequence that is more or less in proportion to the gravity of the offence. We hope God thinks this way, too. Thus, we tend to comfort ourselves with the belief that our sins are "not too serious," and, therefore, we

*Sin and the Sacraments*

hope our punishment will not be too great either and our relationship with God not too badly damaged.

But the devil is not interested in justice at all. Sin means we are dropping our guard; we are stepping out from under God's wings that protect us. Given such an opportunity, Satan will smack us as hard as he can—you can bet on that. I'm sure there are divine constraints: God's mercy, our guardian angels, and our faith (see Ephesians 6:16), and Satan knows that, if he is too obvious, we would catch on to his game. However, the bottom line is that we should have a strong motivation to avoid sin and do the positive actions that God wants us to do.

In the Old Testament, we see the concept that sin often resulted in illness and suffering. It might have been due to original sin, the sin of the suffering person, or the actions of someone else. There is definitely a strong thread to this effect; even while the book of Job makes it clear there is more to the story. For example, Psalm 106:13–15 and 28–29 makes the point that illness was the result of sin for the Hebrews in the desert. In fact, the forty years they spent in the wilderness was because of their hardness of heart. The converse, that blessings and good health result from adherence to righteousness, also appears in the Old Testament: Psalm 103:11–18 and Exodus 23:25–26 are two examples.

In the New Testament, Jesus also alludes to this belief and declares that repentance is necessary to prevent calamity:

> *At that time some people who were present there told him about the Galileans whose blood Pilate had mingled with the blood of their sacrifices. He said to them in reply, "Do you think that because these Galileans suffered in this way they were greater sinners than all other Galileans? By no means! But I tell you, if you do not repent, you will all perish as they did! Or those eighteen people who were killed when the tower at Siloam fell on them—do you think they were more guilty than everyone else who lived in Jerusalem? By no means! But I tell*

> *you, if you do not repent, you will all perish as they did!" (Luke 13:1–5).*

Jesus seems to be indicating that, because all people are sinners, we are all open to suffering and peril, which is the result of sin. The best antidote is repentance; repent before the peril can overtake you. Other New Testament Scriptures focus on death as the ultimate result of sin.

This is not meant to be a universal answer to the issues of evil and suffering. The Church is very wise to state that the only adequate answer to the question of evil and why evil exists is the totality of the Christian faith (see *CCC*, 309). The point here is simply that this dynamic makes sin—even venial sin—dangerous, very dangerous. Clearly there are other dynamics that lead to suffering: persecution for faithfulness to God and *"so that the works of God might be made visible through him"* (John 9:3, speaking of the man born blind). However, personal sin is one of the key causes of suffering, both for oneself and others.

In the example I shared above, there was no obvious connection in the physical or intellectual realm between my venial sin and my depression and anxiety; the connection seems to have been only in the spiritual. In other cases the connection may be more obvious, as when sin creates strained relationships with their resulting internal stress. Stress is well recognized as generating physical, mental, and emotional suffering in many ways. Sin is certainly a pervasive source of illness, calamity, and suffering in the world, especially the heart crushing suffering caused by true evil. However, much is also at work to redeem and protect us: God's mercy, forgiveness, and his ability to bring good out of evil for those he loves. When the hour is really dark, remember:

> *This is for me like the days of Noah:*
> *As I swore then that the waters of Noah should never again flood the earth,*

> *So I have sworn now not to be angry with you, or to rebuke you.*
> *Though the mountains fall away and the hills be shaken,*
> *My love shall never fall away from you nor my covenant of peace be shaken, says the LORD, who has mercy on you.* (Isaiah 54:9–10).

The Catechism tells us that sin dulls our understanding and makes it easier to sin more (see *CCC*, 1865). With a history of sin, what we consider small or insignificant may, in fact, be much more serious than we perceive. This is frequently true with addictive sins such as excessive drinking, drug use, swearing, or pornography. If we clearly perceived the damage we are doing to ourselves, to others, and to our relationships, we would have a much stronger motivation to stop. In addition, a guilty conscience is a distraction when one is trying to pray, praise, or otherwise serve the Lord. Beyond this, sin also impacts the effectiveness of our ministry when we have a guilty conscience. The *Catechism* says, speaking of venial sin, *"It impedes the soul's progress in the exercise of the virtues and the practice of moral good"* (1863). It *"allows charity to subsist, even though it offends and wounds it"* (1855).

An old teaching compares serving the Lord with trying to run water through a pipe: the water is the grace of the Holy Spirit which we (the pipe) are directing to the proper place. If the pipe is dirty and corroded on the inside, not much water can move through it. Conversely, as we increase in holiness and become more Christ-like by following the Lord, the pipe becomes clearer and more effective.

## The Sacraments—Personal Encounters with Christ

Now the bright side of the coin: while sin may lead to more trouble than we suspect, it is also true that the sacraments can be much more effective than we usually recognize. Picture yourself as a servant in the household of the Lord. The Lord has been away, but now he returns. On his way to the house, he stops by the fence where you are busy making repairs. He smiles broadly. He asks how you are doing. Is the work going well? How are the sheep? Need any supplies? This is the master-servant relationship couched in love, mutual respect, and affection. This is what (or should be) happening each time we participate in one of the sacraments. It is a one-on-one, personal encounter with the Lord. The *Catechism* puts it this way:

> *By means of the words, actions, and symbols that form the structure of a celebration, the Spirit puts both the faithful and the ministers into a living relationship with Christ, the Word and Image of the Father, so that they can live out the meaning of what they hear, contemplate, and do in the celebration (CCC, 1101).*

Sadly, for many Catholics there is little Christian education past adolescence, so they remain stuck with an immature understanding. As is to be expected with children and young people, the view of the sacraments that develops is overly simple: a ritual process one goes through with a predetermined outcome—typically the minimum grace and blessing the Lord wants to bestow. Unfortunately, all too many of us remain bound to this process-oriented concept of sacrament, failing to make the transition to a realization of the personal encounter with God that occurs.

But if we approach each sacrament as that faithful servant, rising from our work and greeting the Master by the fence, communicating our needs and concerns, the difference can be dramatic. God is not bound to providing the minimum graces. He can and will do significantly more if our spiritual condition is one of expectant faith, we are eager for the fulfillment of His plan, our need or His love and affection calls for it. Often this takes the form of some flash of understanding and appreciation about one's relationship with him or, possibly, an instance of healing. For example, I recall one Mass near Christmas years ago. I had been contemplating how long ago Christ's birth was when, suddenly, I realized in a deep, interior way that the Mass itself is a timeless event and my participation in it was no less than that of Peter, James, John and the others who were at the first Mass nearly 2,000 years before. I have a number of friends who have seen visions of halos, auroras, or angels during Mass. Such flashes of insight or special visions deepen our appreciation of God's goodness and love for us.

## The Healing Power of the Sacraments

With regard to healing, the Church teaches very clearly that healing is a possible outcome when we approach the sacraments as a personal encounter with the Lord. As the *Catechism* states:

> *Often Jesus asks the sick to believe. He makes use of signs to heal: spittle and the laying on of hands, mud and washing. The sick try to touch him, "for power came forth from him and healed them all." And so in the sacraments Christ continues to "touch" us in order to heal us (CCC, 1504).*

In my case one such healing was totally unexpected, yet it came. I was at a weekday Mass, feeling absolutely miserable with a bad head cold. That was before going up to Communion. After Communion I returned to my place in the small chapel, knelt down, and realized I was healed. All my symptoms were gone! Similar healings have happened to friends of mine, and I am sure they are relatively common, not just with the Eucharist but with other sacraments as well. One friend shared with me how, years ago, his young son was near death from viral meningitis as a result of the measles. The boy's fever could not be controlled, and the doctor felt sure they were going to lose him. Their parish priest, who was with them at the hospital, asked to go in and see the boy. Rather than give the child the Anointing of the Sick, the priest confirmed the boy. Twenty minutes later he was sitting up in bed, eating Jello, completely healed. Go figure!

The Church is quick to point out, correctly so, that we may not always receive a physical healing; the healing may also be spiritual or intellectual. Of course, realizing the close connection between sin and suffering discussed above, this distinction fades. The immediate healing will most often be spiritual, with intellectual and physical good health to follow gently later. Many of us fail to understand the complexity and time-consuming nature of the healing process, and thus we fail to perceive God's healing work.

For example, consider a person with back problems, the result of years of poor posture, heavy lifting, or certain types of exercise. God's healing tends to be very deep and complete; he is not only concerned with the immediate problem. He will work to bring about a change in that person's habits as well as heal the symptoms and current damage. Instantaneous healings—we call these "miracles"—occur when God wants to make a special point about his love, mercy, power, or the truth of a particular teaching. Otherwise, the healing is likely to proceed gently and take some time. God may also involve what appears on the surface to be purely natural processes. For example, he might enlighten our minds so we understand the cause of our ailment and can thus prevent its reoccurrence; he might give especially keen insight to our doctor, or he might simply accelerate the natural healing process.

God's idea of healing might also be quite different from ours. I have a relative with one foot larger than the other by two shoe sizes. Healing for her came the day she was shopping for shoes and noticed another girl about her age also looking for shoes in pairs. It turned out she also had one foot larger than the other—the opposite foot—and wore the same sizes! Ever since (and it has been many years), whenever either of them needs shoes, they just buy two pair and ship the two they can't use to the other person.

Let me provide one more example from my personal life related to the sacrament of penance and habitual sins. You know the kind of

*Sin and the Sacraments*

sin I mean—those nasty habits virtually all of us struggle with at some point in our lives. The more serious include addiction to drugs or alcohol, gossip, indulging in pornography, to mention a few. The struggle against them can cause significant disturbance to our spiritual peace, and the bondage can be incredibly difficult to break. Often the struggle can last for years, as mine had. We might find it virtually impossible to resist the temptation when we are not at our best—overtired, upset, or lonely. The best advice I can offer in such a situation is to realize that it's God who must break the bondage for you. Make a commitment to him that shows you are serious. Tell him you will do some special, positive thing; something extra each day (or once a week) to show him you are serious about wanting the bondage to this sin broken. It might be praying a rosary, fasting, or attending daily Mass. This is simply a way to fight the problem when we are at our best instead of at our weakest.

In my case, the bondage was broken very unexpectedly one day when, on a business trip to Albuquerque, I went to a weekday Mass and confession. I didn't know the priest, of course; he was from Pakistan and about to leave for a new assignment later that day. During penance, I confessed my struggle with this particular sin, and, in addition to giving me absolution, he prayed over me for a few moments, either in a Pakistani language—or maybe it was in "tongues." At any rate, the bondage was broken then and there, never to return.

Patience and faithfulness is what is required from us. The power for victory comes from God, typically when least expected and most often from penance, the Eucharist, or one of the other sacraments. Speaking of the Eucharist, the *Catechism* says:

> *It is a remedy to free us from our daily faults and to preserve us from mortal sins (CCC, 1436).*

Certainly the Eucharist should be regarded as the prime remedy for healing the effects of venial sins—all the effects including impediments to our *"soul's progress in the exercise of the virtues and the practice of moral good"* (CCC, 1863), and the suffering, in whatever form, from our merited punishments.

In spite of the Church's teaching, these kinds of spiritual experiences may not seem real or expected by many of us. It doesn't match our normal experience in the Church and in our secular culture; we'll take a look at this issue in the next chapter.

**Key Takeaways**

- Sin is very dangerous, the source of much suffering.

- The sacraments are person-to-person encounters with Jesus, and great, but often unexpected, graces flow from them. They are there to help us accomplish our joint mission with God.

- God's healing power is manifest in the sacraments, but it is often not instantaneous. Don't fail to recognize it simply because it takes a little time, or when it includes natural, or what appear to be natural, processes.

- A positive focus on our mission and service to God is one of the most effective ways to overcome our sinfulness, especially habitual sins. Failure to do good when we have the opportunity is also a form of sin. When we focus our efforts to grow spiritually on service—not just for God **but in union with God**—we will minimize suffering, both ours and that of others.

## For Further Reflection:

- Psalm 119:1-16 — There is great joy in following God's law and many blessings from being proactive.
- CCC #1863 — Effects of venial sin
- Romans 3:21-26 — All men have sinned, but they are saved, not by the law, but by Jesus Christ.

## Chapter Five

# __Ruts in the Road__

*I have told you this so that you might have peace in me. In the world you will have trouble, but take courage, I have conquered the world (John 16:33).*

Growth in faith is a key element, probably *the* key element, of spiritual growth. Thus we began in the previous chapter looking at sin and the sacraments in a way that was intended not only to foster a deeper understanding but also to build some hope and expectant faith so you will more directly experience God's love. Knowing what to look for is very helpful in being able to perceive God's work, and perceiving His work increases one's faith. As your faith increases, more channels open for God to work, so the whole thing becomes a cyclical "pull yourself up by the bootstraps" process. God uses each little effort we make to build our experience, and thus our faith, so the next time round we can respond better. More on that later. First, though, let's pause and take a look at the question of perception.

Unfortunately, most of us have grown up in a society that has not served us well in enabling us to perceive spiritual realities. Much of what we believe, what we expect will work or not work and what we perceive as real or probable, we learn from our environment, from our culture. In the practical, secular sense, this works quite well since our understanding and perception is derived extensively from the physical environment in which we live. Thus, most of our decisions are based on fairly accurate perceptions, at least in terms of physical realities. That's the basic way humans operate.

However, in seeking to grow spiritually, we must move into a different environment, transforming the secular world and exchanging it for the Kingdom of God. All of us in America, at least to some extent, start from a place which is "out in the weeds" in a spiritual sense because we have grown up learning the lessons of a culture that is often hostile or indifferent to spirituality. Many of these attitudes, perspectives, and ideas go back generations. Some are rooted in the fact that we (both Catholic and Protestant) are in a Western/Roman church culture with its emphasis on a rational religion, as compared to an Eastern/Orthodox culture with its greater emphasis on mysticism and spirituality. (Not to imply one is better than the other; this just shows one source of the anti-spiritual bias.)

In Western culture especially, science has been very successful over the past few hundred years in making countless improvements in technology and lifestyle. This has led to a very strong bias toward reliance on the understanding of reality almost exclusively in scientific and physical terms, discounting spiritual explanations. A second strong influence in American culture is humanism, the idea that human ideals and potential are what really matter—there is no higher authority over man, and man can achieve anything to which he sets his mind. With this perspective, ideas of absolute truth, especially spiritual or moral truth, quickly fade; all "truth" becomes relative, the object of each person's preference. These forces work together to discredit belief in an absolute morality, revealed spiritual truth, and God in the biblical sense. In practice they form a strong incentive to retain a secular mindset, a mindset that diminishes our faith in the things we need to know and practice to grow spiritually.

Here are three examples of specific perspectives we should watch for and be on guard against. Keep in mind that these are cultural patterns that, while generally pretty common, tend to run in some localities or groups of people and not others. Also, each person's upbringing and personal strengths and weaknesses can make these issues very problematic for one person and not at all for another.

- First is the deist idea that God is remote—that he does not interact with us as individuals. For the true deist, the belief is that God created the universe, got it up and running, and then just left the scene or lost interest, leaving us here to fend for ourselves. Even among church-going Catholics (and, I would suspect, other Christians), this idea is found in diluted forms. One is that, while God might providentially provide for us, hear our prayers, and eventually save us when we die if we avoid serious sin, he does not speak to us or guide us individually.

One fellow parishioner, speaking of Abraham Lincoln, said, "It may have been good he died when he did—he thought he could hear God. He was probably going insane." Similarly, some of my children's school friends who experienced spiritual awakening during their high school years also quickly found their parents becoming concerned that they were "losing it." Another friend, at prayer before the Eucharist, sensed a reminder to check a list of things she needed to do. She dismissed it, thinking it was a distraction. The omission of an item from the list soon led to an embarrassment. It didn't occur to her until it was pointed out that it was probably God providing the "distracting" reminder while she still had time to fix the problem. The reality of personal relationship and communication with God is a deep thread running through Christian spirituality, but it certainly cuts against the grain of American culture.

- Second, there is cultural pressure to avoid public prayer or other formal recognition of God. People don't want to be labeled odd or different. This is the pressure that makes many of us reticent to make the Sign of the Cross or say grace before meals in public. When some sad event is brought to our attention in the workplace, we have the ubiquitous "moment of silence" rather than a moment of prayer. We now say "Happy Holidays" instead of "Merry Christmas." This is where the long, slow, bitter culture war is fought. *Culture* by definition is "public"—we could call it the public belief system. When God disappears from the public view, the war is being lost, and the struggle to draw close to God is ever more difficult.

- Finally, there is a prevalent attitude that the spiritual dimension is not important, at least not for this life here and now. Outside of the Sunday homily, very little adult education occurs for most people in the Catholic Church. Not that continuing education is not offered, but most people don't take advantage of it. A Protestant friend of mine told me attendance in his church's adult weekly education program is about 87 percent. In our Catholic parish, typical of many Catholic parishes, we would be ecstatic to see 8 percent attendance. This is a serious Catholic cultural problem. It appears that the majority of the congregation believes they learned all they need (or all there is) to know about Christianity when they were children!

Cultural issues also have an effect on the day-to-day practice of what is emphasized and what is not in our churches. The local church is, after all, made up of people who live in the culture, as did their parents and their parents' parents before them. As an analogy, one might think of ruts in a rural country road; like ruts, the culture provides a subtle but continuous influence on the daily choices that are made. Deep ruts and potholes make travel hazardous, slowing the traveler's journey and, perhaps worst of all for our spiritual analogy, taking his concentration away from the goal of the trip and putting it on the rutty road itself.

The perception of sacraments can be an example of this. If we look at them merely as turnkey operations, preset rituals with predetermined results, our attention is drawn to the institutional law and process, which soon creates dryness and leads to a lack of interest. It is not enough to simply say, "This is meaningful." The meaning flows to the person as a result of his or her relationship with Jesus and the burden of discipleship he or she carries. Discipleship creates a real need for spiritual graces, and these are in turn supplied by the sacraments.

The ruts in the road of current American Catholicism—at least those that most affect spiritual growth—often take the form of a "void." Those things that should be taught are simply omitted; those things that should be done or emphasized are not done, not emphasized. The church continually tries to promote spiritual growth, but with little effect. Too often only weak or no positive affirmation of God's power takes place, no encouragement to have expectant faith, to rely on God. I believe this is a cultural habit rather than a conscious decision. Not everywhere, but all too often, church preaching, programs, and even the liturgy seem to have fallen into a comfortable rut that has reached a compromise with secular culture.

The apostle Paul tells us, "Thus faith comes from what is heard, and what is heard comes through the word of Christ" (Romans 10:17). But if the word actively being proclaimed is silent on a topic, then faith does not grow in that area. God becomes limited in what he can do since he is slow to intrude where our faith does not invite him.

## What's Not Being Said

An elderly priest took several minutes, digressing from his excellent homily, to encourage parishioners to call sooner, rather than later, when someone was in need of the sacrament of the anointing of the sick. He came across as a very thoughtful and godly man. However, as he discussed the benefits of the sacrament, he gave no positive affirmation that the sacrament would actually bring healing! Wouldn't a person call all the sooner if he or she had confidence in at least the possibility that the sacrament would speed physical healing?

Two issues are at play here. First, too many of us associate God's healing only with instantaneous miracles. As we discussed in chapter 4, we fail to recognize that God works in all the complexities of the healing process, and, more often than not, he simply steps in to smooth and accelerate what appears to be a natural healing process. Second, if it were just one sermon or one priest, it would not be an issue. The problem is that this seems to be the norm; in my experience, this is virtually the way this sacrament is always discussed. The result is a lack of faith, not just in some individuals, but in the Church as a whole, and without faith the fruits of the sacrament are correspondingly weak.

This example is similar to what happened with regard to the charismatic gifts of the Holy Spirit listed in 1 Corinthians 12 and elsewhere in the New Testament. Here is a very deep rut that both limits spiritual growth and the fruits of a deep spirituality, the very power of the Holy Spirit to build up the Church. In fact, it is so deep, as we shall see in chapter 7, that God has stepped in to repair it in a relatively dramatic fashion.

Again, the issue is silence. Each year these New Testament Scriptures detailing the spiritual gifts are read at Mass, and each time the homily predictably avoids all mention of them. I've been watching this for decades. Similarly, preparation classes and materials for the Sacrament of Confirmation focus only on the Old Testament gifts of Isaiah 11, which describe Christian maturity (wisdom, understanding, counsel, strength, knowledge, and fear of the Lord); the New Testament gifts may not even be mentioned. Partly, this is because preparation for the sacrament is intended to enable us to work maturely, in unity with one another, to carry out our responsibilities in society and the Church, areas where the Isaiah gifts are paramount. But the New Testament gifts are the tools to make us successful, so why are they ignored? Likewise, while I have heard the New Testament gifts addressed in classes for adults entering the Church, nearly always it is without distinction between the natural gifts of healing, speech, teaching, wisdom, discernment, etc., and their supernatural counterparts.

Here's an illustration of just how serious and pervasive avoiding the gifts of the Holy Spirit has become. A friend of mine was attending weekly Mass, and the Gospel reading was from Mark 16, "These signs will accompany those who believe…." (driving out demons, handling serpents, laying on of hands, and healing the sick). Since the group was small, the priest asked if anyone there believed that Scripture. My friend was the only one to respond affirmatively. Along with the crowd, the priest said he didn't believe it either! Here we have a long-standing Catholic teaching—rooted in Scripture and early Church history, witnessed to by many saints with healing gifts (St. Bernard, St. Dominic, St. Vincent Ferrer, St. Martin de Porres, and St. Don Bosco to mention just a few) that has effectively fallen out of Catholic teaching in the practical sense.

The cultural issues discussed above have a serious effect on spiritual growth, effectively constricting the flow of grace and the power of God, both in prayer and in the sacraments. It is the cumulative effect that is so damaging. Our culture has become one of weak faith and little expectation that God will work in a practical and immediate way. Even the elementary practical wisdom of how God works is missing. How should we pray for his intervention, and what should we expect? How does one discern a prophesy[5] or word of knowledge[6]? How can we recognize when God is speaking?

Encouragement and opportunity for personal witnessing about the spiritual life is also lacking. Rather than create the problem, this rut tends to inhibit the cure. Enabling a person to hear testimonies of how God has worked in the lives of others, especially in the lives of

---

[5] Prophesy is a spiritual gift whereby a person speaks "for God," that is, on God's behalf, under the inspiration of the Holy Spirit. Typically the message is one that builds up, encourages, or provides solace to those who hear.

[6] Word of knowledge is knowledge of a hidden factor or insight into some aspect of faith that comes by inspiration from the Holy Spirit rather than by experience or study. Examples are when Jesus knew Nathanael had been sitting under a fig tree before Philip called him (John 1:48) and his foreknowledge of his death and resurrection. A more complete discussion of the spiritual gifts is found in chapter 7.

people we know and respect, is one of the most effective ways to encourage each other's faith. Unfortunately, there is little opportunity for such sharing in the day-to-day life of a Catholic parish—certainly not for the "once a week" Catholics, and not much more so for the active parishioner. Here we have a clue to a possible path forward—and also a challenge. God is not only interested in encouraging our individual spiritual growth; he is gravely interested in the growth of the entire church.

An important contributing factor we should note is: people love simple, clear-cut answers, even when the question is neither clear nor simple. After all, we are all busy. Why dig into details and complexity when a simple answer will do? Why pull out the recipe book, collect all the ingredients, and mess up the kitchen when you can open a box and stick it in the microwave? The silence discussed above makes it easy for people to rest in their laziness.

Such a simplistic approach is the appeal of some non-Christian religions: they promise the benefits of a religious life but don't demand too much. Even within Christianity, many people are happy with a simplistic answer and feel no desire to search further. Jesus' first answer to the rich young man ("You know the commandments," referring him back to the law and the prophets) has that nice simple ring to it, even though we know, upon reflection, that it is neither a simple nor an easy thing to do. Here is the trap, the "easy" answer that many of us fall into. We don't take the time for that extra reflection. The rich young man senses, correctly, that there has got to be more to the answer, and Jesus then gives it. This fuller call, I would argue, even with its greater commitment and demands, is a much easier path to follow than the apparent simple answer. The difference is the grace and power that flows from the Lord. What first appears difficult on the surface is not necessarily all that demanding. Recall Jesus' words: *"For my yoke is easy and my burden is light"* (Matthew 11:30).

It is hard to overestimate how damaging these cultural biases really are. Spiritual growth and the spiritual life itself require faith, and that means trusting in God. One must step forward, make a decision, take an action, perhaps open oneself to ridicule or loss, all based on the simple conviction that this is what God wants. How difficult it is to develop the confidence (faith) needed to take such a step when we are raised in a culture with strong social forces that discount the reality of the spiritual, or associate it with insanity or, at best, being odd!

## In Conclusion

The key point here is that we live in an environment that is hostile to our spiritual lives and our spiritual growth. Like the proverbial weeds, it obscures our vision (and with that our understanding), and it sucks away the nutrients and crowds our growth, restricting our action. The antidote is to be found in the Christian virtues, especially faith and courage, humility and a teachable heart. Faith particularly, in the sense that we always can have confidence and rely on God when we are trying to do his will. From such faith we must draw the courage to act even in the face of obstacles. Likewise we should foster humility, understanding and remaining aware of our own limitations. When we keep in mind that we may not be seeing clearly, we tend to move forward more thoughtfully and more lovingly. God is most likely to use our love to bring forth good fruit and often does so even when our wisdom fails. Lastly, pray for a teachable heart and invest time and energy in your religious education. The prayerful reading of a good spiritual book is a powerful tool in the hands of the Holy Spirit.

## For Further Reflection:

- John 7:37-39 — Come to Jesus for the living water, the Spirit.
- Romans 5:1-5 — The Holy Spirit gives us the experience of God.

- John 17:25-26 (NIV) — *"Righteous Father, though the world does not know you, I know you, and they know that you have sent me. I have made you known to them, and will continue to make you known in order that the love you have for me may be in them and that I myself may be in them."*
- John 15: 7 and 16; John 14:12 — These scriptures describe the link between bearing fruit and answered prayer.
- Luke 9:23 — We are called to take up our cross each day.

## Chapter Six

## <u>Let the Journey Begin</u>

> *But now, thus says the LORD, who created you, Jacob, and formed you, Israel: "Do not fear, for I have redeemed you; I have called you by name: you are mine. When you pass through waters, I will be with you; through rivers, you shall not be swept away. When you walk through fire, you shall not be burned, nor will flames consume you." (Isaiah 43:1–2)*

If the "weeds and ruts" of the preceding chapter along with the apparent depth and demands of God's call on your life has you a little discouraged and downhearted just now—*fear not*. It is good news that follows. Down here in Alabama where I live, the forests and weeds grow so thick you can't see more than a few feet ahead of you, let alone pass through. However, in our spiritual journey we are going forward God's way, so the situation is very different than it appears to our human eyes. What we perceive as an insurmountable obstacle can be easily swept aside in some cases or overcome with training in others. Sometimes it will be a struggle, but whatever the situation, it is all in God's plan. Our task is to simply be attentive and follow the Lord's guidance as best we can. As we do this, we will actually experience and come to understand how the Lord works, and that will build our faith so we are prepared for the next step: understanding comes from doing. This is the first and perhaps the most important lesson to learn.

> *"For my thoughts are not your thoughts, neither are your ways my ways," declares the Lord. "As the heavens are higher than the earth, so are my ways higher than your ways and my thoughts than your thoughts." (Isaiah 55:8–9, NIV)*

## Keys for a Joy-Filled Journey

As you move forward, you will find many reasons for encouragement and even joyful expectation. Here is a short list:

- *God rejoices that you are making the journey.* Whether you're the prodigal son or the faithful servant that has done well with his talents while the master was away, he rejoices that you are making the effort and focusing on him.

- *God created you for the specific journey you must make.* He foresaw the road ahead, and he has given you the natural gifts and talents you will need. The rest he will supply through others or supernaturally. When Jesus sent his apostles out into the towns and villages to proclaim the Kingdom and heal the sick, he instructed them to take no extra cloak, no money, no traveling bag (see Luke 10:4). For God's work, God supplies what is needed.

- *You may not have far to travel.* God has been guiding you all of your life by his providential means and by guiding your perceptions of situations prior to key decisions. Sure, we all make mistakes along the way, but God uses even our mistakes for our good.

- *The path forward is one of learning and growth.* God doesn't expect us to do it all at once. Most of us tend to be impatient and feel we are not making enough progress. That is why keeping a journal is such a good idea: it lets you look back and see how far and how quickly you have actually come.

- *The power for the journey comes from God; it is a supernatural grace.* Often we don't need to destroy the weeds or move the obstacles ourselves. Rather, we respond to God's direction to step to the right place, and then God moves the obstacle or opens a door just at the right time. We simply step through it. In the Old Testament, the Exodus from Egypt is an instructive example. Like the Israelites, we just need to be standing by the shore at the right time, in the right place, with the right people. Somebody will raise a staff; the waters will part, and all we will need to do is walk forward onto the dry path, mastering our fear of the waters piled high on either side. Not a no-brainer, but not all that difficult either. Remember, the people that made that journey had been prepared by witnessing the ten plagues God had sent before their release by Pharaoh.

- *Growth is not measured by human standards, but by God's.* Thus, we don't need to move mountains, raise the dead, or speak to the multitudes. Your progress is measured in terms of inner peace, knowledge of and confidence in God's love, an understanding of yourself and the tasks God has called you to do, growth in holiness, and increased joy as the power of sin in your life is diminished. *A key point: with time you will come to see the progress, the good fruit, and this is very encouraging and faith-building. Ask for the gift of seeing the fruit of your decisions and actions.*

- *Many others have made this journey before us.* If we figure five generations per century, and twenty centuries since Jesus began the Church, that's a hundred generations of accumulated wisdom and the working of the Holy Spirit. There is much we can fall back on.

- *You will meet others along the path who will lift your heart and give you joy.* The solitary aspect is mustering the courage and resolve to set aside your personal plans—and, on occasion, even what appears to be your personal welfare—and follow God's plan, trusting in him. Beyond that, the journey is seldom solitary. Rather, it is characterized by the hallmarks of the Kingdom: friendship, hospitality, love, and joy. Jesus promised his disciples an abundance of companions (see Mark 10:29–30).

- *Jesus, through the Holy Spirit and according to the plan of the Father, will make the journey with you.* They love you and make the best of companions.

This list should be sufficient to give you hope that we really are looking at "good news" and the journey is going to be rewarding.

True, great struggles are to be expected, because we are called to enter into Jesus' struggle against "the world"—that is, the evil of the world. But struggling on behalf of Jesus, with him as your companion, leader, and teammate, is very different than suffering under the weight of sin. That's a path we want to avoid as much as possible. We will encounter the need for self-discipline, training, and the occasional pruning, but in all these cases the fruits should quickly become evident, usually within a few months. The benefits become manifest in terms of greater faith, confidence in God, and the joy of knowing the work is really worthwhile and that you have pleased him.

To begin the journey you must start from where you currently are; there is no other way to do it. Wherever that is, we all start with the same basic first step. If you have made this step before, fine; renew it, and then move on. The step is this:

## Step One: Identify Yourself as a Servant of God

This means a commitment to make the journey of being Christian, to fulfill your baptismal promises, and, most of all, to be a servant of the Lord Jesus. *Servant of Jesus becomes the definition of who you are.* With this focus and this commitment, all the rest falls into place. Your service to Jesus now becomes your number one priority. It is basic to who you are. Whatever was on your priority list before (spouse, family, job, sports, self, money), they all slip down a notch due to this new (or revitalized) number one. Don't worry, though; the rest of the list does not disappear. You still have your life and responsibilities. However, henceforth you are committed to making all decisions from this new perspective. From now on this becomes your fixed reference, the baseline from which life is viewed. As such, because it is in line with God's will and his plan for you, in time this self-identification becomes a source of great confidence and blessing. It is the unique expression of God's truth for you.

To make progress from this point, and to mitigate any fears that you have just signed up for a life of misery, keep these two key points in mind:

1. Being Christ's servant is not a commitment to any preset, cookie-cutter plan; rather, it is a unique

position in the household of God set up for you, and you alone.

2. You are a servant to a person, a person who loves you very deeply and knows you intimately. He knows what you can do, what you fear, and what makes you happy. The relationship is person to person, not person to institution, not person to contract or law.

If you are single, you may fear you will be called to a religious life as a priest or nun. (I recall being in this position once myself.) Such a fear is actually a deception, an effort by the evil one to impede your progress. Again, the commitment to be made is not to *a particular path*, rather it is to *a person* you will journey with whatever the path. You have entered into a relationship of personal service to the Lord himself. The initial path ahead must focus on growing that relationship and learning how to execute that service faithfully and correctly. Eventually, it will lead to some significant ministry, to meeting some significant needs, but it begins by being faithful in small things (see Luke 19:11–19). For some the path might lead to an ordained or sequestered religious life, and those people will be greatly blessed in that vocation. However, the majority of us will have other callings.

Years ago, I was very passionate about the pro-life ministry. (Too passionate, actually—I didn't have the right gifts, and I expect such a ministry eventually would have given me ulcers and made me hard-nosed.) Along with a group I was committed to working with, I went through a process of discernment, eventually coming to the conclusion that pro-life work was not to be our ministry. I have always felt blessed that, first, I could limit my involvement to small acts of support, and, second, the work we did do soon raised up people who handled the pro-life work very effectively. Praise God for *his* plan, not mine!

One more very important point about this commitment to be God's servant: it needs to be public. Not TV and radio public, but public among your friends and family. Let the people close to you know about your commitment to Christ clearly and directly. Just as God created the universe by his Word, so our word makes it a truer reality.

This also helps to avoid the typical New Year's resolution problem: many good intentions soon forgotten and ignored. If you tell your spouse, your pastor, a friend or two, you are now putting your word, and yourself, on the line. At times these people, just by the fact that they know and you know that they know, will help you stay focused on this path you have chosen.

In all God's work, in the Church and in us, both a physical and a spiritual reality combine together. The physical and spiritual are inseparable attributes of the one reality, even though we may speak and think of them somewhat separately for purposes of teaching and understanding. As we proceed on this journey of spiritual growth, we shall see this as a constant factor: physical changes and growth always accompany, sometimes leading, sometimes trailing, spiritual growth. Our spirituality will include a normal, healthy relationship with the Church and community, as well as a normal, healthy physical lifestyle.

**Step Two: Wait and Watch**

When we talk about embarking on a journey of spiritual growth, it might seem strange that the second step is simply to "stop." However, this step is not "stop, do nothing"; rather, it is "stop, wait and watch." It is similar to hunting in the woods. If the hunter begins walking, even stalking slowly and carefully, unless he is extremely skilled the game will most likely hear or see the hunter and flee long before the hunter sees the game. Instead, the wise hunter finds a good position (step one) and simply waits and watches carefully for the game to appear.

For us it is the slightest breeze—the Holy Spirit—that we wait for. This is the crucial skill that must be developed to support and maintain spiritual growth, recognizing that slight movement, the small gesture or sign in a situation that is the beckoning of the Spirit. This capability of recognition is actually a learned skill, and it may seem a little slow and difficult at the beginning. However, you are now in the right position with the right focus for your attention; this is where the Holy Spirit has been drawing you all along. He is indeed anxious to guide you and teach you.

*Let the Journey Begin*

"And I tell you, ask and you will receive; seek and you will find; knock and the door will be opened to you. For everyone who asks, receives; and the one who seeks, finds; and to the one who knocks, the door will be opened. What father among you would hand his son a snake when he asks for a fish? Or hand him a scorpion when he asks for an egg? If you then, who are wicked, know how to give good gifts to your children, how much more will the Father in heaven give the holy Spirit to those who ask him?" (Luke 11:9–13).

To our untrained spirits, it may seem that nothing is happening. The understanding and actual sense of recognition may come weeks or even months later, but it will come. Be assured, however, that the Holy Spirit knows what you can perceive and understand, and the journey *is* moving forward, at least in the spiritual realm if not yet in the physical. Hans Urs von Balthasar points out that it is logically inconsistent to believe that we were created to serve God or even to say yes to faith in any way, and yet believe that we cannot hear him or otherwise receive his guidance.[7]

Let's look at the example of the hunter in a little more detail. Your first step, your commitment to be a servant of Jesus, puts you in the right place in the spiritual sense. You are on the right piece of land; your hunting license is in good order, and the Master of the Hunt will be driving some game your way. However, you should pay attention to some practical things in the physical realm:

- *Just as a hunter makes an effort to be aware of what is happening around him, you must pay attention to the spiritual environment.* Several times throughout your day, briefly stop what you are doing, be quiet, and "listen" for the Spirit. Ask yourself, *Is this what I should be doing? Is my spirit peaceful? If not, does something else need my attention at this time?* If your spirit is peaceful and nothing else comes to mind, thank God for his blessings and go back to the task at hand. The whole process takes about fifteen seconds. You simply are giving the Lord a few moments to allow him to draw your attention to where it is needed. This is a basic prayer. Ask the Lord to help you

---

[7] See Hans Urs von Balthasar, *Prayer* (San Francisco: Ignatius Press, 1986) p.34.

cultivate this habit. The busier your day, the more important it is to take these few seconds to check in with "the Boss."

- *In the morning, or whenever you plan your day, be sure to include a time for quiet listening as just described.* Take a bit more time and mix in some Scripture reading— usually just short passages—and other forms of prayer. Keeping a journal can be a useful tool.

- *A wise hunter will always bring a lunch in case the time spent in the woods is longer than expected.* Likewise, you need to have sources of spiritual nourishment. Attend Mass each week (daily if possible). Build time for some spiritual reading and Scripture study into your week. Even when this seems not to bear much fruit at the time, this activity builds a spiritual "bank account" that comes back to bless you when you need it later. It also demonstrates your commitment as a servant of God in the physical realm and thereby helps you to maintain that focus.

- *Keep your gear clean.* Repent of any wrongdoing and utilize the Sacrament of Penance regularly. This step is extremely important because it brings your spiritual life into the light of the objective standards of Church, scripture and wise council. As for all of us, you are bound to have areas of understanding where you were improperly taught or formed by experience, areas where you have been or can be deceived. While some people are too lax, others are overly scrupulous. The Sacrament of Penance is perhaps your best antidote against these forms of hidden difficulty and sin.

- *Give some attention to your environment — your home and clothes, your art and music.* Your environment should speak of goodness and holiness, not evil or disorder. You want to be living in the Kingdom of God here and now, and your environment should begin to reflect that reality. Not everything in your environment needs to be specifically Christian, but there should be elements that honor God and nothing should honor evil.

*Let the Journey Begin*

- *Don't try to anticipate what God will guide you to do, but be ready to do spiritual works.* His ways are not our ways, so anticipation is seldom useful. You are here to support God's plan, so expect him to do the heavy lifting. Your role is just to contribute. Expect to be led to share your faith with someone, witness to the truth, pray with someone for a specific intention, or counsel someone who needs help. In serving God, expect to enter the realm of charismatic gifts (see 1 Corinthians 12).

The above list contains the essentials of a nominal, day-to-day Christian life. Much of the rest of this book is about learning to recognize and then respond to the promptings of the Holy Spirit. In the next chapter on discernment, I'll share some tricks of the trade in seeking out his guidance. The chapter after that is for those of you who are impatient, who want to immerse yourself in a "school" for spiritual growth and thereby grow as quickly as possible, helped by the example, instruction, and companionship of others. Otherwise, the process is more do-it-yourself and therefore slower, clouded by more uncertainty. Either way works as long as you keep trying. God is highly efficient! In any case God's path forward is unique to each person.

Spiritual growth has two basic components. The first is *recognizing* and then *following* the guidance of the Holy Spirit. This enables us to do good and bear fruit for the Kingdom. The second is *avoiding sin* or, to say it positively, *growing in holiness*. Both require our attention, effort, and cooperation, but in reality both are works of the Holy Spirit. He initiates; we respond.

I emphasize the first of these, the recognition component, for three reasons: 1) It is very encouraging and faith-building once we start to see some fruit; thus it helps us to retain our focus and advance quickly. 2) It is easier — most of us find the second component, avoiding sin, very difficult, especially when faced with heavy and persistent temptation, or temptation in an area where we are habitually weak. 3) Much of the growth in holiness actually occurs over a period of time by replacement – good habits, good lifestyle changes, and good environment gradually replacing and crowding out the habits and lifestyle that lead us into sin and poor choices. Thus, it makes sense to focus on recognizing God's voice and serving him well; it is easier to do and it leads naturally to growth in holiness.

## In Summary

Prior chapters focused on the key elements of spiritual growth, i.e., the development of our personal relationship with God. This relationship begins and always remains one between Master and servant, although it will grow in intimacy and love. This chapter began with a look at the reasons why it is such a good relationship. Not only is it meaningful and full of love, it is also doable and tailored specifically to you. Then we discussed at some length the two key attitudes we must maintain to be successful in this relationship: 1) keeping the relationship top priority, and 2) focusing on communication and responsiveness to the Lord. Note that these are the basic elements that keep any relationship growing and healthy. How we best respond depends on the specifics of the situation, whether it's in marriage or any other relationship, but these attitudes are always needed to keep a relationship healthy and growing. Clearly more should be said about the practical aspects of communication, and we turn to that in the following chapter.

## For Further Reflection:

- Mathew 25:14-30 and Luke 19:11-27 — These passages describe the servants' role while the master is away.
- 1 Corinthians 7:17-24 — Continue in your state of life according to God's call for you.
- Psalm 103 and Mark 10:29-30 — Discipleship has both cost and benefits.
- John chapters 14-16 — We have struggles in the world but unity with the Holy Spirit.
- 1 Corinthians 12 — Accept and expect the charismatic gifts of the Holy Spirit.

# Chapter Seven

# Guidance and Discernment

*Set up road signs; put up guideposts. Take note of the highway, the road that you take. (Jeremiah 31:21, NIV)*

A very common question is, "How can I know what God wants?" Similarly, "How can I know I'm hearing God and know it is him?" These are not questions with short answers. God guides and speaks to us in many ways. Different people are more attentive to different forms of communication. We first must recognize (discern) what we hear as coming from God. This then requires further discernment to determine the correct course of action.

Situations differ; some require just the slightest nudge from the Lord and the path ahead is clear and easy. Other cases involve many clues and competing interests and have much at stake; these require careful discernment and testing. In this chapter, I'll approach the topics of discernment and guidance primarily from the perspective of determining the course of action God wishes us to take. The term *discernment* may also be applied to seeking understanding of oneself and the internal spiritual struggles with which one must deal; the discussion of chapter 9 will be helpful for this second application.

## Discernment Involves Reason

Our objective, of course, is to come into unity with God's will. The first key concept to understand is that *discernment is a matter of reason*. Each of us is subject to many emotions, moods, and a multitude of external and internal pressures; any of these may or may not contain clues from God as to what he calls you to do. However, discernment—i.e., making the correct decision—is an act of the will and therefore a function of reason. Discernment includes sorting out which clues/communications are from God, followed by a decision about when and how to respond. However, any decision should be reasonable, corresponding with what we know about Jesus, Scripture, and Church history and teaching, as well as what we know about the world. At times God's direction will be contrary to worldly wisdom. When discernment leads us that way, we should not fear that path; however, we should do so with understanding and with our eyes open.

To begin, several "guideposts" or points of reference should be considered when deciding whether a certain course of action is reasonable for us spiritually. This is God's passive guidance. The guideposts are warning signs; cross them at your peril. We will also explore the dynamics of active guidance. Passive guidance, coupled with our reason, is designed to keep us out of trouble and point us in a good direction, but it is not specific enough to bring us tightly into sync with the Holy Spirit. More active guidance is needed so we can know when to take a specific action—whether it be a lifestyle change, act of ministry, or some other action which expresses God's love and builds up the Church. There are practical steps to help tap into this more active discernment. As you incorporate them into your daily life, God will use them to provide more specific guidance. Eventually, this will lead us to the recognition and use of the spiritual (charismatic) gifts of the Holy Spirit.

**Take Up Your Calling**

As baptized Christians we have received the Holy Spirit, we are God's own people, his servants. By design we are enabled to perceive guidance from God. We have a place in his household and responsibilities to fulfill. Note, however, that the Lord of the house, our master, is not prone to micromanagement. In truth, he is always there with us (see Psalm 121, to mention one of many scriptures). But our perception is often that the opposite is true; we have the sense is that he is "away." We find ourselves working, or worrying, a problem and the Lord seems to be nowhere near.

In many ways this is not very different from going to work at a normal job, assuming you have a very good boss. Normally, you know your job. You walk in at 8:00 in the morning, sit down at your desk, and begin working from where you left off the day before. As a rule you don't need to go in and ask your boss what you are supposed to be doing, because you know your responsibilities. If you have a wise boss, he or she lets you handle the job in your own way, but he will quickly step in when you ask for help.

God has placed us in a position which we are competent to handle without micromanagement, and he leaves it like that. In reality, God has been training us to think "like him" over the years of our discipleship to him, so we know how we should act. Therefore, do not expect active guidance for each question you face; God expects you to use your brain and your understanding of his ways. Active guidance comes as a result of God's compassion and love for us or to bring about a specific result, but when it is not needed, he does not provide it. When something arises that is beyond our competence, he is at hand, ready to help resolve the issue when we ask, but we are expected to keep doing the work we are capable of doing. Remember, when we are in a jam, God may (and frequently does) resolve it by guiding circumstances or other people, instead of by directly guiding you. With practice, you will learn to perceive the patterns.

**Guideposts Mark the Way**

As you walk with the Lord, seeking to grow spiritually, here are some practical guideposts for your journey.

*Your actions should be compatible with Church teaching, especially Scripture.*
This is an obvious key guidepost. Obey the law of love, the Ten Commandments, lawful authority, and the like. Centuries of experience by millions of people have shown this, invariably, to be the smart thing to do. The hard reality is that following this guidepost may come with a significant price to pay in the short run, while the benefits come later and are often more important to society than to the individual. For example, if you take a moral position at your place of work that ends up costing you your job, the loss of employment can result in significant struggle, at least for a time. Faith is needed that, even when the short-term pain seems devastating, the long-term benefits will confirm the wisdom of heeding this guidepost. Jesus clearly warns us that at times we will suffer loss because of the

*Guidance and Discernment*

Kingdom, but we can trust his love and providence to see us through.

However, a few words of caution might be in order here, especially for significant, life-changing decisions. For instance, following a divorce, a woman stayed away from the Eucharist for twenty years, even though she continued to live a celibate life and remained faithful to the Church. For whatever reason, she simply did not correctly understand Church teaching relative to that situation. Religious education *is* important. Make sure you fully understand what the Scripture and the Church really teach; a single Scripture verse or even the opinion (especially if casually expressed) of a single priest or minister does not necessarily reflect the full truth about the question at hand. There are also certain cases where Church teaching allows for exceptions to be made, or where the local bishop or priest has the latitude to handle a situation differently, as a pastoral matter. A person's responsibilities, his or her competence, who is in authority, and other special circumstances play a role in complex decisions and affect which scriptural truths and Church teachings best apply. This is the reason for the Church's marriage tribunals and the slow and cautious annulment process. The bottom line? Remember that God can find ways where the human mind cannot. Also, be aware that impatience is likely your worst enemy. Give God time, consider all the options, and strive to be at peace with God and Church.

### *God expects you to fulfill your day-to-day responsibilities.*

Normal responsibilities flow from your position in life—care for your spouse and children, going to work and being productive, voting, paying taxes, and the other responsibilities of citizenship and community. These also include the responsibilities that flow from your Baptism: prayer, attending Mass each week, contributing to the Church, concern for the poor, and so forth. Much is to be sorted out here in terms of relative priorities, timing, and approach. That discussion is coming. For now the point is simply this: keep your responsibilities in focus as you decide what the right path is. Like the scripture passage at the top of the chapter says, *"Take note of the highway, the road that you take"*. Pay attention to what you are doing and how it affects your responsibilities and other people.

## *The best test of a course taken is the fruit it bears.*

Here is a guidepost that both helps us in discernment and builds our faith and confidence as we walk with God. Several elements are the key to how it works. With respect to major decisions, the real life-changers, it is fortunate that in many cases there are ways to try out the new path without making a lasting commitment. Dating before marriage, the novitiate stage of entering a religious order, and the hours of practice, education, and training prior to entering into an occupation or learning a skill are all examples. As you embark on any new path in life, keep careful track of the fruit it bears. Does it bring you a sense of peace, joy, and accomplishment?

Perhaps most importantly: does it bring unity with those you love—your spouse and those who are important in your life? Is it in harmony with the Church? Unity is extremely important because with unity in the family and faith community, it is always possible to make adjustments and then move on. However, if there is disunity, the project will most certainly run into serious trouble and likely will fail in the long run because it has lost the support structure that family and community provide.

One way to look for fruit is to float an idea and see how others respond. Are they supportive? Keep in mind that frequently a person will correctly discern a problem but not the solution, or someone may discern the correct path, fully or partially, but not the correct timing. Always take the perceptions of others seriously; even if you don't follow their advice, some adjustment to your own thinking is most likely needed. When others are opposed to your idea, it is often because they perceive the situation differently than you do—perhaps better, or perhaps not as well. It takes self-discipline, but raising an issue and then allowing time for consensus to develop almost always leads to a better path.

## *Are your actions loving?*

God not only always acts in love, he *is* love. Love is his essential nature. So, if you are to grow spiritually, you must grow in self-giving love. "I give you a new commandment: love one another. As I have loved you, so you also should love one another" (John 13:34). Again

*Guidance and Discernment*

and again we are called back to the cross in order to accept responsibility for the mission God has for each of us. This means self-discipline and often self-denial to assure we are primarily focused on doing what is good for others and not worrying about what is good for us.

An important note: "love", as we use the term here, has nothing to do with feelings. Feelings come *to* you; you hardly control them. Agape love comes *from* you; it's a decision of the will about what is really for the good of another person. A young child may look as cute and charming as ever as he or she plays in the yard, but when that child heads for the street, it becomes time for discipline that will likely hurt the child's feelings as well as yours. (If the "child" is a teenager or adult and the "street" is alcohol or drug abuse, the same principle applies.) At times true love can be hard as diamond!

**Practical Steps for Discernment**

The above guideposts are points of reference to guide our reason as we decide what is a good direction and what is not. Guideposts apply to all discernment, but they are the most helpful with the difficult decisions that need to be thought through carefully. In addition, we can do practical things—and God does practical things—to keep our focus on our mission and responsibilities in the Kingdom. These are tools that train us to pay attention. They help us notice when the Lord is "passing by" or when the Holy Spirit is "speaking." Typically they do not involve great decisions or anything that involves serious consideration. Rather, these practical steps lead to simple communications with the Lord; the Holy Spirit might nudge us to check on a friend, go to a particular place for lunch, pray for someone, remember to pick up something at the store, or the like. These are simple, practical things that put us in the right place to do something to build Christ's kingdom, help someone else, or allow God to bless us in some way. Terms frequently used for these nudges from the Holy Spirit are *promptings* and (less accurately) *leadings,* small inspirations that create an opportunity to serve God.

The guidance that results from these simple steps can, and often does, help with the more difficult and complex guidance issues, but in these cases they generally work together to form a pattern over time. For example, it is often difficult to discern what constitutes your vocation, i.e., your mission for the Lord. But if you look back at the little things God has prompted you to do in the past, you see what has borne good fruit and what has not. In reviewing the work God has used you for in the past, you will often see a pattern that clarifies your gifts and points forward toward the work the Lord wants you to continue to do.

## *Prayerfully ask the Lord to show you the fruit of your decisions.*

This is a prayer God has answered many times for me, much to my blessing. As we have just discussed, looking at the fruit is a particularly appropriate method of discernment when dealing with questions of deciding when to make a change in some activity you are doing. As you go through life, you will be called to many activities for a time, but not forever. At first an activity may bear good fruit and you have a passion for the work, but eventually the seasons change, and the time comes to move on to something else. Passion for the work is one of the good fruit indicators, a sign that God wants you doing that particular thing, but when passion turns to a sense of being burdened and you feel stale, leave that work to others and move on to whatever God has in store for you next.

At one point I had a very difficult decision to make about relocating to another state. One Sunday after Mass, I took some extra prayer time and asked the Lord to show me the fruit of staying where I was. As I left the sanctuary, I bumped into another parishioner, a little old lady who said something to the effect that my family and I had been a great blessing to her and her husband. Like I said, God has often answered that prayer for me, but this holds the record for the clearest and quickest response. We didn't move for this and other reasons, but this event was a great help in the discernment process.

## *Pause to recollect what you are currently doing and what you should be doing.*

As you go through the day, especially each time you finish a task and before you start another, pause and reflect briefly on what you are doing and why, and what else needs attention. Simply strive to be a thoughtful person, not one absorbed in distraction and emotion. The

*Guidance and Discernment*

important aspect is keeping who you are—God's servant—firmly in the forefront of your mind, ready to serve in whatever situation pops up. Such a pause gives the Holy Spirit a chance to bring another task, more urgent or of higher priority, into your mind.

## *Ask for doors to open.*

This aspect of discernment typically comes into play when a person already has indications they are being led to some fairly significant lifestyle change: changing jobs, moving to a new home, or taking on a new responsibility. The basic idea is to ask God to confirm his guidance by confirming the reasonableness of the new direction. For whatever reason, you have already begun to think that God wants you to make the change, but uncertainty, potential risks, or significant obstacles still exist. Simply ask God to confirm his guidance by "opening a door"—i.e., sweeping away one of the risks or obstacles, perhaps by a certain date.

For example, if you are considering taking a new job, then you might ask for a certain condition or benefit for your family. In other cases you might ask that your current home would sell by a certain date or for a certain price; or that you are able to drop a current responsibility so that you have time to pick up the new one. The process of asking God to open a door is best used for serious matters, when we need a check against fulfilling our responsibilities. Blessed Teresa of Calcutta often worked this way. If one of her sisters came forward with an idea to improve the ministry, Blessed Teresa would direct the sister to investigate what resources were needed to implement the new idea, and then they would pray for the resources. If the required resources showed up, they would move forward and implement the change.

A word of caution here; not all open doors lead to where the Lord wants you to go. Praying for a specific door to open as part of a larger discernment process is one thing, stepping into an open door that just happens to be there is quite another. Rely on your reason and the guideposts; promptings and open doors primarily help with the timing and confirmation of a decision.

## *Perform a "fleece test."*

This approach to discernment was inspired by Gideon, one of the more interesting characters in Scripture. His story is found in Judges 6; it is a short and important story. Gideon knew full well what God was asking him to do—he was just afraid to do it. Gideon took a woolen fleece and laid it out on the threshing floor overnight, asking God to confirm his guidance by allowing the dew to fall on the fleece but not the floor around it. That is just what happened! Just to be sure, though, he asked God to do the opposite the next night to eliminate any possible error in his supposition. A fleece test is asking, as a sign, for some highly improbable event to occur. I should point out that this is not a highly recommended process for seeking guidance. For one, it seems that people who tend to use it, like Gideon, already know the answer. If you know the answer, a more basic objection is that it is putting God to the test—a sign of lack of faith and perhaps presumption. Remember, Gideon had a lot on the line; he was putting his life at risk as well as those of his followers. God might not be so tolerant of our weakness if we are just discerning what contribution to make to a particular charity.

## *"Promptings": hear God's voice directly.*

Hear we step into the specifically charismatic dimension of Christianity. Much of what we need to know about this topic is summarized in 1 Corinthians 12-14. Promptings are supernatural, the direct work of the Holy Spirit given to draw us into unity of action with Jesus and thus the Trinity. They take a variety of forms, but typically they are just a thought, sense, or idea that pops into our minds. Whatever the form, they are a clear and immediate expression of God's love and guidance. The direct beneficiary of this gift may be the person who receives it, or it may be given to one person for the benefit of another, to build up the Church. In any case it is a supernatural expression of God's love for us.

Keep in mind that until one is practiced in hearing God speak and recognizing his voice, most likely the promptings will seem very natural—just another idea popping into one's head. Even after years of experiencing these leadings, there will still be times when it is not immediately clear if a particular prompt really is from God.

*Guidance and Discernment*

Remember, man was designed and created to be able to have this communication; it is part of the destiny for which we were created. It is the voice of the master speaking to his servant. When Jesus told us to "watch," this was what he meant. When you sense a prompting, you ask yourself, "Is this what Jesus wants?" Then respond accordingly.

The graces that flow from promptings range from the powerful and dramatic to the very gentle and common. To give you an example of the former, not long ago I heard the testimony of a fellow I had hired to do some work on my house. He said, once while he was at work, he sensed a very strong need to go home immediately. Dropping everything, he rushed home to check on his family. Running into the house he found that his wife, an invalid, was okay. She said their young son had gone out to play. Quickly checking the back yard, he could barely hear a call for help. The boy had fallen part way into a well that had been covered by a broken-down shed next door. Fortunately the boy had been able to hang on long enough for his father to come and rescue him. Later investigation revealed the pit and shed were full of poisonous snakes!

Much more typical was a gentle prompt I felt while working in the yard, that I should stop and pet my dog. She was a *very* old dog that we had had since she was a puppy. She was loose because I was there with her and she seldom wandered far. Later I realized that she was gone, and it turned out she had wandered into a neighbor's yard and died. Sadly, I had not taken time to give her a pat on the head, so I missed my chance to give her a proper goodbye. Even with years of experience, it is all too easy to miss God's gentle voice.

If the idea of promptings is new to you or you lack faith that God works this way, then it is much easier to miss this grace, like the case we described in chapter 5; the friend was "distracted" while praying by the thought that she should check a list of things she needed to do before Mass. She missed something in preparation of the altar because, not expecting that God would work this way, she ignored the prompt. I am afraid this reaction is all too common. *If you don't expect God to communicate with you, if you have no faith that he works this way, you will likely miss it.* We are talking about paying attention to the small, still, natural-seeming voice of God.

## Gifts of the Spirit

Guidance-related gifts form a substantial list, and their operation is very specific to individuals and situations. In addition, certain of them are very similar, so it can be difficult—and perhaps unnecessary—to make clear distinctions between them. The following will at least give an idea of the scope of how the Holy Spirit works in this area.

### *Perceptions and Ideas:*
When you walk into a situation or perhaps read something (especially in the Bible), God will often direct your mind and observations. This can feel completely natural, so don't strive too hard to perceive where the supernatural begins and ends. For example, as you step into a business meeting, you might notice a co-worker pulling a couple of aspirin from her purse. You know she suffers from migraine headaches, so, instead of taking your usual seat at the back of the room, you sit at the table to do what you can to support her and relieve the pressure of the meeting. In other cases you are faced with a problem and, suddenly, the solution is apparent. When we go through the day with the Holy Spirit within us, who is to say where the idea comes from or where the line is drawn between what is his work and what is ours?

### *Wisdom in discourse:*
This is the gift of first perceiving and then being able to express wisdom for a specific situation. Often this gift comes to those who are called to teach or preach, but it can also be manifest in a casual conversation. Once my wife encountered a couple fellows promoting a church revival as she left a local store, so she invited them to an event we had coming up at our Catholic parish. When she received a quick, negative response about "you guys worship Mary," she replied along the lines of, "No, Mary was only human, so we honor her but we don't worship her, although I suppose a few folks get carried away. We're careful not to dishonor Jesus' mama." Before the fellow could respond again, his comrade stopped him saying, "You know she's right; we have some folks like that in our church too." Clearly the side comment about "a few folks get carried away" was from the

*Guidance and Discernment*

Holy Spirit and set the common ground so the exchange was friendly and useful while generating mutual respect. Probably wisdom in discourse is most commonly encountered in the confessional and comes from the Holy Spirit's gift of counsel active in the priest.

## *Knowledge in discourse:*
This gift is very similar to the preceding one, but where wisdom is really a form of deep understanding, the gift of knowledge is revelation of specific facts. The recently sainted Padre Pio had this gift, and it contributed greatly to his ministry. When hearing confessions he sometimes knew a person's sins without having to be told.

Once, when I was shopping for a new vehicle and having a hard time making a decision, the Lord gave me direct knowledge of the price to offer. The salesman took the offer, and I purchased a good vehicle that gave us years of good service. Another example still makes me wonder. One evening my wife and I were playing Yahtzee with a young friend of the family. Yahtzee is not a game we care for, but our friend was really keen to play. All evening the Lord kept showing me which dice to pick up and which to leave. The patterns didn't make sense, but my score was astronomical. Don't ever try to beat the Lord at dice!

Some years later I used this as an example in a teaching. Afterward my wife said, "Oh, I remember that night. He kept telling me, too." However, my wife figured that would be cheating and would hurt our friend's feelings, so she ignored the prompt. I'm sure an important lesson is in there for somebody, but I've never figured it out!

## *Faith:*
The word *faith* has several meanings within Christian culture, from "the Faith" that signifies the composite body of Church teaching to "faith" in the sense of trust and confidence in God. Here, and in 1 Corinthians 12:9, it means a specific gift of trust for a specific situation—for example, the grace to be able to face very difficult circumstances (perhaps surgery or death or other loss) with confidence in God's mercy and love. This gift is also especially

important in situations that require boldness and taking a risk. Is there a better example than Jesus accepting death on the Cross?

## *Prophesy and other forms of hearing God speak:*

Prophesy is literally "speaking for God," so it frequently occurs in a prayer meeting or other gathering of Christians. The Holy Spirit communicates a message to a person, who then shares it with those present. Alternately, the person may receive the communication at an earlier time, most often during his or her prayer time, write it down, and then share it later. This latter approach is perhaps a bit weaker because part of the power of the prophetic word is its newness—it is the "now" or *rema* word, meaning the right thing said at just the right time, often with a sense of surprise. If the prophesy is valid, what is said is never contradictory to Christian tradition, but how it is expressed, the timeliness and wisdom of the message, can have power to move hearts and bring significant change. At the very least, it brings a sense of peace and faith that God has the situation under control.

There can be great variety as to how God communicates with the prophet. The following is a list of the most notable, and these also can be considered as separate gifts, each unto itself. The method the Holy Spirit chooses varies from situation to situation and person to person.

- **Word for word:** God may communicate the whole message in word-for-word fashion, almost as you would hear another person speak (although the prophet has no perception of sound—the words just enter the mind), or it may only be the first few words. Then, when the prophet begins to speak, the entire prophesy just flows forth.

- **Word of wisdom:** The Lord may just give the understanding of what the message needs to convey, and the prophet then expresses it in his or her own words.

- **Word of knowledge:** The word of knowledge is similar, but the message is a precise fact—for example, the number of a song to be sung or Scripture to be read. Something I regularly do is to quiet my spirit early in my morning prayer time and listen for a number. When a number pops into my mind, which it invariably does quickly, I read or pray the psalm with that number. Over and over the Lord has blessed me in this way, the psalm being the very word I needed for guidance or encouragement that day.

- **Visions:** In this case the understanding is communicated "visually"; an image or picture flashes across the screen of one's mind. For me the vision always seems to be very quick, just long enough to convey the idea. However, it would not surprise me if other people saw longer visions, even "movies."

- **Scripture passages:** You are reading Scripture as part of your prayer time, and suddenly one verse or passage jumps out at you. You just know God is saying those lines to you that day. Very similarly, it may be a line from a liturgy or the Sunday homily. Some priests, I'm told, receive complements for the power and meaningfulness of their words even, on occasion, for a line they never spoke! The Holy Spirit must be filling in. Another variation is "seeking a passage," usually some variation of closing your eyes, sticking your finger on a page at random, and reading the verse where your finger falls. I know that doesn't seem highly spiritual, but God knows and loves us, and I know many folks that have been helped in this simple way, myself included.

- **Tongues with interpretation:** Sometimes, during a time of silence in a prayer meeting, someone will speak out loudly and clearly in an unknown or foreign tongue, which then is followed by another person (occasionally the same person) giving the "interpretation" in English (or whatever language everyone there understands). In some cases the interpretation is the expression in English of what was actually said. In other cases, what was spoken is a prayer requesting a prophesy, and the "interpretation" is the prayer being answered. In still other cases someone present will have the charismatic gift of interpretation of tongues and will be able to give an interpretation. One friend of mine with this gift told me about some friends of his from the Middle East who were joking with him in Farsi. He surprised them greatly by understanding the joke. The gift of interpretation extended beyond the prayer meeting in this case.

- **Dreams:** Besides being the result of too much caffeine, pizza, or bad movies, dreams can also be a form of communication from God. We awaken, remembering the message and at least part of the dream with the sense that it may have been from God. Like the other communication gifts we have been discussing, it is probably easier for God to get the message through to us when our minds are relaxed, in a peaceful listening mode, and sleep can provide that. However, when we wake up, we usually sense holiness or significance in the situations when God speaks, which helps to assure us it is really him speaking and we were not just having normal dreams. Many scriptural examples exist of God speaking in dreams, the most notable being Joseph, Mary's spouse, and Pharaoh (who needed the other Joseph to interpret for him).

As you can probably see from this list, much of the initiative for God's guidance comes from God himself. Our part is to be watchful servants. "Watchful" means being attentive, expectant, prayerful people who give time to quietly waiting in the Lord's presence. Being "servants" means that we are willing to respond positively to the guidance we receive. God is not going to waste his time giving us guidance we plan to ignore. Communications from God and prophetic words can come spontaneously, often when you least expect them, or as a result of praying for a word, or when a prayer group leader asks for it, calling for a period of silence and listening for the Lord to speak.

It's important to note that all these methods of God's guidance are *tools* of discernment; discernment itself is the work of the will and reason—understanding and deciding how to put the guidance (communication) we have received into action. Weightier matters often require discussion with those we love, our co-workers, and

*Guidance and Discernment*

those in authority over the situation. Seeing a good spiritual director is always recommended. If the matter is significant, the discernment process can be expected to take time, testing, and, most of all, looking for the fruit.

For small matters discernment can and should be very quick: you pause, consider the guideposts, and ask yourself if you are comfortable that it was from God. Yes? Then respond. You ***will*** learn to recognize the Lord's voice. Just like the voice of a friend on the phone, on occasion you might wrongly identify it, but ninety-nine times out of 100 you get it right. Trust in God. He is not just your guide; he is also your teacher, your protector, your helper, and your co-worker. Be bold. Remember that inaction when God is calling for action is another way of getting it wrong, and often the opportunity does not come again anytime soon.


**For Further Reflection**

- Psalm 123:1-2 — How to pay attention to the Master.
- Jeremiah 31:7-14 — The Lord guides, shepherds, and blesses his people.
- 1 Corinthians 12 to14 — The gifts and working of the Holy Spirit and the character of true love.
- Judges, 6 and 7 — Read how God called Gideon to deliver Israel from the oppression of the Midianites.
- "Living Things, Collected Poems" by Anne Porter, Zoland Books. — Many useful examples.

## Chapter Eight

# Traveling in the HOV Lane

*They devoted themselves to the teaching of the apostles and to the communal life, to the breaking of the bread and to the prayers. Awe came upon everyone, and many wonders and signs were done through the apostles. All who believed were together and had all things in common; they would sell their property and possessions and divide them among all according to each one's need. (Acts 2:42–45)*

High Occupancy Vehicle (HOV) lanes are a common sight on freeways entering and leaving many cities. For the city it reduces traffic problems; for the commuter it speeds travel and lessens the danger of the daily commute. From the beginning, as the scripture above indicates, the Church realized the same thing—traveling together reduces the hazards and speeds the journey. For all of us, the primary community we live and grow in typically includes our families, friends, and parishes. These generally are a "mixed bag" in terms of spiritual growth. They can be a great support to our growth one moment and then, moments later, present us with obstacles. I'll present a few ideas about dealing with obstacles in the next chapter. In this chapter, we'll focus on spiritual communities—and one in particular that can provide a great resource to support our spiritual growth.

Throughout Church history there have been many "ecclesial communities," as they are now called: groups of people banding together for a common vision and with a common goal within the Church. Several monastic movements, the Friars Minor (Franciscans), Order of Preachers (Dominicans), and the many orders of priests and religious come to mind as early examples which are still active and fruitful today. In today's parish the layperson is likely to find people active in several ecclesial communities. Cursillo, Marriage Encounter, Kairos, the St. Vincent de Paul Society, Third-Order Franciscans, and various Marian movements seem to be particularly active in my area. It is important to realize that, while each community develops a culture of its own which tends to be unique to that community and its mission, each community also has deeper underpinnings to the Gospel message itself which need to be recognized and fostered within the entire Church. Thus ecclesial communities serve to spiritually benefit both their members and the greater communities in which they are immersed.

Ecclesial communities differ substantially in their goals, visions, and spirituality, but I believe it is fair to say that all of them contribute to a person's spiritual growth. I say this simply from my experience with several of them and the fact that they are communities attempting to do God's work. Of course, how much they contribute depends on many factors: the vision and goals of the community, the community's size and activities, and the commitment of the members, not to mention the maturity and gifts of the leadership. Just the fact that they are communities brings several factors to bear that encourage spiritual growth:

1. The members experience the reality of God's work; they become doers of the Word, not just hearers.

2. The continual contact with the community's work sharpens and helps maintain a person's focus on the need for spiritual growth and especially on the need for God. It is in the day-to-day attempts to serve him that we really come to understand how much each of us needs him.

3. The members learn to rely upon and support one another; the strength of one alleviating the weakness of another. In the wisdom and interaction of the team, we often get our best view of God's wisdom and grace.

4. Community prayer supports and encourages all of the above.

The individuality of the spiritual growth process is something that needs to be understood and appreciated. It is one of those little paradoxes of Christianity that our involvement in community should also support and increase our individual strengths and talents. The work and even the problems of the community give a person the field to labor in and the testing ground for works of faith. Faith must be exercised in order to be strengthened. In ecclesial communities, spiritual realities and graces lead to physical and temporal blessings in the lives of real people.

Just as God loves each of us as individuals, his call to deeper union with him is very unique and individually planned for each person. We all seem to find it easy to respond to and follow God in some areas of our lives and much more difficult, or even impossible, in others. Not only human weakness comes into play, but our training and culture make a big difference in our ability to respond. One such aspect is our struggle for holiness. List sixty ways to tempt a good man, and he will simply brush aside nearly all of them, but with one, or perhaps two, he will really struggle and often fail to do right.

Individuality also occurs in respect to channels of grace. I know of two priests, for example, who were very godly men trying to do their best for the Lord. In both cases they were exceptional preachers. Their listeners could not help but sense the Lord's wisdom in their words—words that moved the heart as well as the mind. However, for a long time both had a great deal of trouble believing in the authenticity, at least in their current situations, of the charismatic gifts, such as prophesy and healing. In both cases the Lord eventually stepped in and revealed the reality of these gifts to them. One of these priests was someone we knew personally here in town; he served at a neighboring parish a number of years ago. The other you will recognize: St. Augustine.

Being God's servants, the key questions are, as always, what is God calling us to do to encourage our spiritual growth and what is he calling us to do to further his plan for the salvation of us all? Involvement in an ecclesial community is typically one of the best ways to grow rapidly and answer both these questions. Minimally, strong involvement in at least the general communities (family, parish, and neighborhood) is necessary for spiritual growth and bearing fruit; exceptions to this rule are very rare. Of course, to benefit from any community requires a certain level of involvement and commitment. Therefore, while involvement is strongly encouraged, this is a decision that requires discernment before

*Traveling in the HOV Lane*

jumping in too deeply. Be bold in testing the waters, but let the lessons of the preceding chapter come into play. Fortunately, becoming involved in an ecclesial community is (or at least should be) a step-by-step process so one has time to experience and evaluate the fruit.

## The Catholic Charismatic Renewal

The particular ecclesial movement that has meant the most to my wife and me, having been involved in it for over forty years now, is the Catholic Charismatic Renewal, (or the "Renewal", for short). There are a number of reasons why I think this is a very important community:

1. It is probably the most general and powerful of the current ecclesial movements. Since its beginning in February of 1967, it has touched approximately 10 percent of the Church worldwide. It appeals to people of all cultures but especially the poor and people of the third-world countries.

2. It strikes right to the heart of spiritual growth, activating the graces of Confirmation and opening a person to direct communication with the Holy Spirit.

3. There are two major fruits that flow from the charismatic renewal:

    a. Experience, understanding, and use of the New Testament gifts of the Holy Spirit, including wisdom, knowledge, healing, prophesy, tongues, and others listed in 1 Corinthians 12.
    b. Largely because of the personal experience of these charismatic gifts and the actions of the Holy Spirit, there is significant deepening of one's faith and love of God, the Church, and the sacraments.

4. Over the years I have known many people who have become involved with the renewal for several years and then moved on to very effectively serve in other ministries. Other times we see practices that originated within the movement flowing

into parish use. Thus the fruits of the Renewal continue to spread and enhance virtually all aspects of Christian life.

5. Perhaps the most important reason of all is that the Renewal is not so much an organized movement as a revival of the basic spirituality of the Church. There are, to be sure, a variety of charismatic organizations including national and international coordinating committees, covenant communities, various specialized ministries, diocesan liaison offices, and many local prayer groups. However, these are only loosely interconnected; the main connection is the sharing of wisdom and teaching between the groups. Guidance and oversight, in the temporal sense, comes primarily from the local church. The real guidance that gives unity and direction to the movement is from the Holy Spirit working individually with each person and group.

## The Baptism of the Holy Spirit

Before we look at the graces that flow from the Renewal, we had better take a moment to define a term that is used a great deal within this movement: Baptism in the Holy Spirit. This is a scriptural term, appearing in the synoptic Gospels where John the Baptist spoke about the promised outpouring of spiritual power that Jesus would bring about at Pentecost. The word *baptism* itself means "saturation" or "soaking," the way one soaks a piece of cloth in a vat of dye to change the color. Thus the grace of Pentecost is to saturate a person with the Holy Spirit. When baptized in the Spirit, a person becomes aware of the Spirit's action in his or her life, and there is direct communication and awareness of the Lord's presence on an ongoing basis. It is also a grace that activates the charismatic gifts, as the events of that day and Peter's speech in Acts 2 indicate:

> *Then Peter stood up with the Eleven, raised his voice, and proclaimed to them, "You who are Jews, indeed all of you staying in Jerusalem. Let this be known to you, and listen to my words. These people are not drunk, as you suppose, for it is only nine o'clock in the morning. No, this is what was spoken through the prophet Joel:*

> *'It will come to pass in the last days,' God says, 'that I will pour out a portion of my spirit upon all flesh.*
>
> *Your sons and your daughters shall prophesy your young men shall see visions, your old men shall dream dreams. Indeed, upon my servants and my handmaids I will pour out a portion of my spirit in those days, and they shall prophesy.*
>
> *And I will work wonders in the heavens above and signs on the earth below: blood, fire, and a cloud of smoke. The sun shall be turned to darkness, and the moon to blood, before the coming of the great and splendid day of the Lord, and it shall be that everyone shall be saved who calls on the name of the Lord.'*
>
> *...Peter [said] to them, "Repent and be baptized, every one of you, in the name of Jesus Christ for the forgiveness of your sins; and you will receive the gift of the holy Spirit. For the promise is made to you and to your children and to all those far off, whomever the Lord our God will call."* (Acts 2:15–21, 38–39)

Thus baptism in the Spirit is to be equated with the graces the Church calls forth with the sacrament of Confirmation since, as the *Catechism of the Catholic Church* states, "It is evident from its celebration that the effect of the sacrament of Confirmation is the special outpouring of the Holy Spirit as once granted to the apostles on the day of Pentecost" (*CCC*, 1302). To understand how all this works we need to reflect again on the individual nature of the spiritual growth process and return to the point we made in chapter 4: the graces that flow from the sacraments are to some extent dependent upon the situation and disposition of the recipient. Thus, the graces of Confirmation are to some extent latent, coming forth later in life as the situation demands or as the individual is ready, all in God's plan. Confirmation is rightly classified as a sacrament of initiation, of beginning. Like a seed that grows, it imparts an "indelible mark" or "character" which "perfects the common priesthood of the faithful, received in Baptism, and 'the confirmed person receives the power to profess faith in Christ publically and as it were officially (quasi ex officio)'" (*CCC*, 1304–1305). This perfection is a process—the process of our individual spiritual growth as well as our participation in the external, visible aspects of God's plan for us. Baptism in the

Spirit thus can be described as a threshold along the path of spiritual growth. Once crossed, the other aspects of spiritual growth—growth in holiness, development of ministry, effectiveness in prayer—all become much easier because faith is continually nourished by the continued awareness and guidance of the Holy Spirit.

There is a serious pitfall in Catholic culture to be avoided; it is the fact that many people come to the conclusion that significant spiritual growth is "not for them." It is in avoiding that pitfall that the charismatic Renewal makes a very significant contribution. Some people fear spiritual growth; many are just not interested; some believe it is not possible for them because they are still sinners, and still others don't understand the concept. Whatever the reason, the possibility of receiving direct guidance from God and of a personal awareness of the presence of the Holy Spirit active within one's personal life is simply dismissed. This is a result of the cultural environment we live in that is so hostile to spiritual growth and spiritual truths in general; it leads directly to a lack of faith.

Even among those of us who do believe, many take a passive attitude and have low expectations of the sacraments, prayer, and other spiritual exercises. Many believers don't take seriously (or don't understand) how essential it is for spiritual growth to accept Jesus as Lord and embrace a servant's attitude. They fail to take the necessary steps: frequent reception of Eucharist, participation in spiritual education programs, Scripture reading, prayer meetings, and reading spiritual books—all of which would provide the spiritual and intellectual nourishment required and put them in the place where they could grow spiritually. Instead these factors combine to maintain and perpetuate the environment of low expectations, weak faith, and spiritual lethargy.

The grace of the Renewal counteracts this pitfall with three realizations, all of which are evident in the people involved:

1. The use of charismatic gifts greatly strengthens weak faith, as does witnessing the use of the gifts by others.

2. Prayer, in particular the prayer of those who have already been baptized in the Spirit, is extremely effective in bringing about the baptism for others.

3. God is eager for all of his people to be baptized in the Spirit. As this passage from Luke's Gospel, as well as the passage from Acts quoted above, affirms:

> *"And I tell you, ask and you will receive; seek and you will find; knock and the door will be opened to you. For everyone who asks, receives; and the one who seeks, finds; and to the one who knocks, the door will be opened. What father among you would hand his son a snake when he asks for a fish? Or hand him a scorpion when he asks for an egg? If you then, who are wicked, know how to give good gifts to your children, how much more will the Father in heaven give the holy Spirit to those who ask him?"* (Luke 11:9–13)

**The Life in the Spirit Seminar**

For years the Renewal has used a very simple teaching series, the Life in the Spirit Seminar, to introduce people to the baptism in the Spirit. The key element is the personal faith-building witness to God's power resulting from the use of the charismatic gifts in the lives of the people present. The basic teaching consists of the two essentials for growth: the Lordship of Jesus and our role as servants. Near the end of the seminar, the leaders and others who are already baptized in the Spirit lay hands on and pray for the baptism to come to those who request it. For those who do not feel ready, there are prayers for whatever struggle the person is facing and for an increase in faith. The seminar also includes a brief instruction on the charismatic gifts since those who are newly baptized in the Spirit begin to experience them in their lives.

This simple approach is extremely effective. Nearly everyone attending the seminar receives a tangible spiritual blessing, and for those who ask for the baptism, most receive it with visible evidence that appears immediately or within a few days. From my own experience, I've observed that many people who enter the seminar as not-very-serious Christians experience a very pronounced change in their lives. Those who have been seriously committed to Christ for a long time experience more subtle effects. In either case, however, the transformation is both tangible and lasting.

A major grace, then, of the Renewal is the rapidity with which it brings about this key milestone in spiritual growth, the baptism in the Holy Spirit. The seminar typically runs for seven weeks, consisting of weekly thirty-minute sessions plus participation in the prayer life of the hosting community. That has proved sufficient to build the faith and understanding of the participants to the point they are able to experience this wonderful grace that has lasting effect. Compared to the years of slow growth and spiritual struggle the typical Catholic-in-the-pew undergoes in order to reach the same maturity, the difference is truly dramatic. Either way the result is the same—maturity in the graces of Confirmation.

The difference is comparable to what I experienced with my gardening. The first time I tried to garden at our new house, six tomato plants proceeded to grow less than eighteen inches that year. In total, they only managed to produce two or three tomatoes; the soil was that bad. One year and a pickup load of manure later, the same number of plants grew chest-high and yielded bags of tomatoes for table and freezer. For both tomatoes and our spiritual growth, the secret is the same—the availability of the right nourishment.

My wife and I took a different path to the baptism in the Holy Spirit. It did not involve a Life in the Spirit Seminar, at least not initially. At the time we were both dedicated Catholics; I was a twenty-eight-year old cradle Catholic, and my wife was a convert from a few years before. For several years, however, I had a persistent list of interlocked questions: Where was the proof for Catholicism? For Jesus and Christianity in general? Yes, the logic of Catholicism all made sense, no complaints there, but where was the evidence? Where was the power? Wouldn't it be nice to see just one miracle so I could *know* that it was not simply some logical and self-consistent construct, but actually a reality?

Remember, God was dealing with a young physicist/mathematician here; I would receive my doctorate two years later. I was fully aware that it is possible to build a self-consistent theory without any real

*Traveling in the HOV Lane*

counterpart. That said, it all changed one weekend when Beth and I went to visit my brother and his wife. They lived about eighty miles from us in Yerington, Nevada, a small town in the middle of nowhere. This was in 1972. My brother and his wife had received the baptism in the Spirit about a year before in April of 1971. Looking back and remembering that the Renewal began in 1967, it's easy to see that it had to be God's hand that spread this grace to such a remote, small town so quickly.

Following Sunday Mass, my brother introduced us to a little old lady who miraculously had been healed of a cluster of five small tumors; prior x-rays showed their presence clearly, but during surgery they found only empty pockets. Empty pockets and dense tumors would have the opposite appearance on x-rays; that I knew. He also introduced us to a very pleasant young family man who was washing his car. As we drove away, my brother said, "He used to be a heroin addict"—a clear contradiction to what we had just seen. Clearly my brother and sister-in-law were trying to build our faith, but it wasn't having much, if any, effect. It happened too quickly, and there was no time to reflect; we were thinking about breakfast.

The change came later that evening just before we were ready to head home. After a very few words of explanation, they asked if we wanted them to pray over us so we would receive the baptism in the Holy Spirit. The logic of my response was pretty thin and simple—if it was from God, I didn't want to turn it down; if not, nothing would happen. Not exactly a great act of faith! Anyway, we agreed; they prayed for both of us, and we hit the road for home asking each other if we thought anything had happened.

The question was resolved within about three weeks. We started reading Scripture, and here or there a passage would stand out to us. Too self-conscience to do it any other time, I started to pray in tongues while in the shower. My wife didn't receive that gift until several years later (while she was helping give a Life in the Spirit Seminar for some teenagers), but a gift of prophesy came much sooner. In a sense the change was subtle, definitely not dramatic, but it was also clear, positive, and lasting. Something had happened with that prayer. For one, there was never again a question in my mind about the reality of Christianity; it was real, and I *knew* it.

To conclude this chapter, let me emphasize two key points. The first is the absolute truth of the passage from Luke 11 quoted above. Like a loving father, God wants, God hungers, to give us his Spirit in the deepest and most abundant way possible. The Spirit comes when we pray and there is faith in the prayer. Part of the great blessing is that the faith of all involved contributes: those who pray as well as those who receive the prayer.

The second point is that the baptism in the Spirit is only a benchmark on the spiritual journey—an important benchmark, but still only a benchmark. There is spiritual growth before it is reached and much, much growth after it has been passed. The nourishment we require is not just needed to achieve the baptism of the Holy Spirit; it is also necessary for our journey of growth. There is no dipping into the spiritual kettle, pulling out a blessing and then walking away unchanged and unchanging. There is a journey to make, and it is best made together, supporting each other, with our fellow Christians, whether you are called to the Renewal or some other community.

**For Further Reflection:**

- Learn more about the meaning of Confirmation and the charismatic gifts by reading "Welcome the Spiritual Gifts!" by Peter Herbeck of Renewal Ministries, also by CCC, 1287–1288.

- You can find doctrinal and pastoral guidelines concerning the baptism of the Holy Spirit and the charismatic Renewal from the International Catholic Charismatic Renewal Services Doctrinal Commission, available from Chariscenter USA (800-338-2445).

## Chapter Nine

## <u>Out of the Desert</u>

*"I have told you these things, so that in me you may have peace. In this world you will have trouble. But take heart! I have overcome the world."* (John 16:33, NIV)

Struggle, pain, depression, anxiety, fear, broken hearts, broken people—the list of the world's troubles seems endless. The first question that comes to mind for many of us is: How do we handle the struggle? However, as important as this question is, it is not something we can tackle head-on within the confines of this book. The sources of struggle are much too diverse and the solutions too varied; these topics are the subject of many books. For those of you who are really stuck on this question, remember that you need not face the struggle alone. God is always with you (see John 14:18–20; Matthew 28:20), and help is available. If you don't know where to turn, start with your pastor. Even if he can't help you himself, he will almost certainly be able to refer you to other resources within the community.

So we come to a second question—one we will tackle: how can we grow spiritually (and why should we try) when we are immersed in a world of trouble? While this, I would argue, may be the less immediate question, it is not necessarily less important. For one thing, spiritual maturity, the objective of spiritual growth, is perhaps our best protection against the struggles of the world. The better we avoid sin and the deeper our faith, the fewer the struggles, and the less deeply they impact us.

Also, on the positive side, we are often more motivated to seek spiritual growth when we are heavily burdened than when the day is filled with joy and blessings. When we struggle we recognize how much we need God. Therefore, if we still do the right things to promote spiritual growth, even in the midst of our struggles, most likely we will grow much more rapidly than at other times. The growth may improve our perspective and help us avoid further mistakes, but it seldom removes the problem immediately. The burden remains, and under that burden, the blessings of the spiritual growth can be hard to detect. Only later, when the struggle and the growth bear their fruit does the blessing become clear.

Traditionally, the agents of struggle are classified into three groups: the world, the flesh, and the devil. In this application, "the world" means the failures of our culture and a secular understanding of the truth, for example, an attitude that the solution for our problems ultimately lies with the government, doctors, education, or some other human institution. While all of these may be helpful, the ultimate source of our salvation is always God. "The world" includes various other misconceptions, such as equating freedom with license or success with power or money. "The flesh" refers to human weakness—most typically some form of instant gratification and pleasure, be it alcohol, drugs, illicit sex, whatever. Lastly, "the devil" alludes to the direct work of Satan and his minions; it includes not only temptations but also the stirring up of unhealthy emotions and deceptions.

Real-world struggles are both complex and frustrating because the solution usually is not readily apparent. Part of not being able to see the solution is not being able to see the root cause or causes—and in many, if not most, situations, more than one root cause is at play. It is here that the elements of spiritual growth are most likely to come to our aid, in identifying and understanding the root problems and in guarding us against them. I'll provide a series of examples, mostly things I have learned from my own experience, which will hopefully serve to illustrate either the connection of struggles with the failure to follow principles of spiritual growth, or conversely, how those principles aided in identifying a solution or avoiding further trouble.

## Headed Off Course

Our poor decisions and responses to situations that lead us off course are usually the product of our temperament and our worldview. Our temperament drives how we make decisions, and our worldview is the concept of what is true that forms the basis for those decisions. Over the years, as we live and grow, our environment, parents and families, teachers and friends, and experiences combine to develop within each of us a worldview, a concept of what is true and important and what is not. However, our worldview is never fully accurate or complete, and so we find ourselves setting priorities and making decisions based on baseline beliefs that are at least partially faulty. If our temperament is such that our emotions play too large a role in the decision-making process, the situation is aggravated. For the cases where the process is well reasoned and the baseline is relatively accurate, or at least accurate enough, we can make good decisions. In other cases we may not be so lucky.

Let me give a small example that is still painful after thirty years. It was a case where my view of what is important badly skewed my priorities. My temperament is such that I really like to see things done right, and over the years I developed an appreciation for having the right tool for the job. The problem arose when I needed a new table saw, and I became obsessed with getting the best one. I wanted to see a European saw that was only available in a few major cities in the US. My chance came on a combined business trip and vacation. I cut my vacation short as I had a few days of work in Los Angeles. My wife and the kids were to fly home from our vacation via Los Angeles, where, my business concluded, I would meet up with them and catch the same flight home.

However, I was determined to stop at a store that carried this particular table saw. The traffic was heavier than I expected, and I almost missed that flight. The stewardess had her hand on the cabin door to close it; once closed I would not have been allowed on the plane! Praise God for his mercy! I don't want to think of the repercussions of having my wife fly home without me, no house or car keys, trying to manage several very young children, and not knowing what happened. Not only that, a few months later on a business trip to Washington, DC, I made much better decisions and *still* almost missed my flight. Clearly my worldview about time margins and priorities during travel was out of whack, in addition to my ideas of what I needed in tools. I was being adjusted, and I needed it. Soon after these events I purchased a good quality but readily available table saw, and it has served me well ever since.

So, how does one avoid such a problem or, having already "stepped in the puddle," extricate oneself with a minimum of damage? I doubt there is a single cure, but the priorities and disciplined approach to decision-making described in prior chapters can significantly help. Looking back at my little episode, I can now see how I was trying to serve myself, not the Lord. I wanted the "best saw," and the telltale signs of anxiety and frustration were present, too. If I had paused to reflect on what I was doing and where my priorities were, the Lord might have been able to slip a word in edgewise, and I could have avoided this painful lesson. Looking back, the Lord was gentle with me.

Another key lesson is to be careful of your attitude, always be aware of the fact that "we know partially and we prophesy partially" as Paul tells us in 1 Cor. 13:9. Even for the brightest human beings, the intellect and available information is too limited to always be right. Aristotle, certainly one of the world's greatest minds, generated what was probably the longest standing error in science, identifying meteors as waves of flame from gasses burning in the atmosphere, the way smoke sometimes burns above a fire. A clever but erroneous idea, it hung around the halls of science for about 2,100 years. Being too confident that we are right is a sure way to end up wrong, perhaps very wrong. The problematic attitude here is basically a form of pride, one of the deadly sins; many are the downfalls it causes. The antidote, humility, means in this case that we are aware of our limitations. We must remember that our understanding is always partial and subject to error, and so we should seek to have a teachable heart, seek counsel whenever faced with a significant decision, and always seek to broaden our education, both formal and informal. And as I learned with the table saw, *the best* is not always necessary—often *good enough* does very well indeed.

## Distraction

Another source of problems that can lead us into the spiritual desert is our current environment and the people in it. It's common knowledge that the young, especially teenagers, are particularly subject to peer pressure, but I doubt this vulnerability ever completely leaves any of us. The people in our lives form our community. A spiritually healthy community is a tremendous blessing. An unhealthy community is problematic, but most of us live in communities that contain a bit of both. Perhaps the question we should ask is how did Jesus deal with his community? Two things stand out:

1. *Jesus was a community builder, drawing and focusing his attention primarily on those who were important to his mission.* To them he had a lasting commitment. To everyone else he was loving and considerate, always reaching out to draw them to himself, but the limitations of his human life meant that there had to be limitations in these relationships. Even to his enemies he was respectful, taking time to answer their questions and bring them face-to-face with the truth, but then he would move on, attending to his own business. Only with his death, resurrection, and the sending of the Holy Spirit did the fullness of his commitment to all these others, us included, become evident.

2. *Jesus led his community.* Like the shepherds of the time, he would walk in front and lead the way, leaving his sheep to follow along behind as best they could. Jesus knew where he was going and what he was doing. He did not let his community distract him from his mission, as the events leading up to his passion and death illustrate clearly. Each of us, like Jesus, has a calling and a mission, and we, too, are called to be leaders in our communities in imitation of Jesus.

The challenge of leadership is twofold. First, we must overcome distractions ourselves so that we remain true to our course, and, second, as we lead we must overcome the fear that our community will not follow. There is always a temptation to look back over our shoulder to see if we have harmed or broken a relationship. *Will they continue to follow? What will happen to them, and to me, if they don't?* The answer is always faith and patience. Stay on the course God has set for you. Godliness, love, truth—all the fruits of following Jesus have great power to attract others as we draw closer to the Lord. However, this power is also very gentle so the short term reactions may be very difficult. Like playing a big fish on a rod and reel, when the fish bites the hook, you just have to let the line run out, having faith that, in time, when it tires, you (or more properly, the Holy Spirit) can reel it in. Our first priority is serving our Master; our concerns for ourselves and others are secondary. Jesus understood this well.

> *Jesus said, "Amen, I say to you, there is no one who has given up house or brothers or sisters or mother or father or children or lands for my sake and for the sake of the gospel who will not receive a hundred times more now in this present age: houses and brothers and sisters and mothers and children and lands, with persecutions, and eternal life in the age to come." (Mark 10:29–30)*

## Brokenness—Yours, Mine, and Ours

With the exception of Mary and Jesus (and Adam and Eve before the fall), all people retain a substantial amount of brokenness until the Lord heals them. It seems basic to the human condition that within each person are areas of great virtue and strength and, within the very same person, areas of weakness, brokenness and perhaps even evil. When sin is added to the mix, the weakness and brokenness grow, just as strength and virtue grow with holiness and service to the Lord and his people. The balance is on the side of the good; after all, each of us is created by God in his image and is loved by him. Both the healing and the sin involve human participation and are life-long processes. Thus it is not difficult to find examples, even extreme examples, close to and within one's own life.

Typically these human traits, both the good and the not so good, remain hidden until an event occurs that brings the virtue or brokenness to the light. Just like a physical sore, a spiritual or intellectual sore produces pain and often a bad reaction when it is disturbed. Thus, the same person is likely to exhibit great strength, compassion, wisdom, and other good traits in many circumstances and yet exhibit the opposite in certain circumstances, depending on where the hidden brokenness lies and what sets it off. If one studies history, one quickly finds historians who point out the failings of the best of us. Likewise, I recall in my professional career, the same manager made the single worse people-management decision that I ever encountered, but also several of the best.

Several observations may be useful:

- *The basic mission of Jesus is to save and heal the whole person.* The Gospels use the same Greek verb (SODZO) to refer to both saving the soul and healing the person. It follows that the best way to be healed is to focus on following Jesus, fulfilling our mission as his servants here on earth.

- *Don't get down on yourself.* You might feel that you are much more broken than the people around you, but the real truth might be that they are just better at hiding their brokenness (not necessarily a good thing), or you are more perceptive of your own shortcomings (that is a good thing).

- When an encounter with someone touches a broken area (either in that person or in yourself), and the result is unexpected and upsetting, be as understanding, loving, and patient as you can. Realize that the pain results from the unexpected contact with the wound, most likely without any conscious ill intent on the other person's part. Approached in a different way, in a different time or place, contact with the same person may be as pleasant and loving as one could ask for. Even more importantly, see the situation exactly for what it is: contact with an area of brokenness. Pray for the person. The brokenness is probably the result of sin—but not necessarily the sin of the person you are dealing with. The sin could have been the action of some third party or society in general. In any case, it is just one more thing the Lord has yet to heal, so pray for the healing and rejoice in that hope. Last, protect yourself and take care not to aggravate the situation by contacting the same sore spot again.

- *Trust we must, but don't trust anybody too much.* When something happens that touches a broken, weak, or evil area in another person, great love can mitigate the negative effect on you. Jesus always has such love, but the rest of us, well, probably not so much. How much love we have depends on many factors, but especially how long and well we have followed the Lord. Particularly when the hurtful encounter happens with someone who "should know better"—a parent, church or civic leader, or role model, the best remedy is to look past the person to the Lord. Put your trust in the Lord. God's good is permanent. All these troubles are passing away. It is the Lord who brings good out of bad situations: "We know that all things work for good for those who love God, who are called according to his purpose" (Romans 8:28). Exercise prudence and patience to help you through such difficulties, and remember God always proves faithful.

- *Jesus may be giving you an opportunity to share in his mission to heal humanity's brokenness.* Consider this fact when such brokenness comes to light either within yourself or others, or both. Jesus may be calling on you to step forward in faith and participate in his mission. Your loving response in the face of brokenness and evil could well be the vehicle God will use to bring the healing. Here, be bold in prayer.

## In the Enemy's Sights

When you are struggling, it is important to keep in mind that the issues are not all about the people and the physical situation involved; we also have a spiritual enemy who is likely to be making a contribution, whether small or great. Satan and his minions are dedicated to making us miserable and leading us astray. Given a bad situation, one of his typical ploys is to play on our emotions, making it difficult for us to think clearly. Guilt, anger, anxiety, depression, hurt, and fear are the devil's stock in trade. One effect of these emotions is that they tend to make us withdraw and isolate ourselves from our community and support. This plays exactly into Satan's hands—the wolf separating a sheep from the flock so it becomes more vulnerable. The antidote is to master your emotions and stay in contact with your community, the Church, and the sacraments in particular.

The evil one works by lies and deception, so keep in mind that he strives to remain invisible and unperceived. It might look something like this: your spouse comes home and says something short and unkind. The reality may be that your spouse just had a rough day, is fatigued, and didn't intentionally mean to hurt you. It was a simple human mistake by someone not functioning at his or her best. However, Satan, the accuser, might bring to your mind prior mistakes of a similar kind that tend to awaken your anger, sense of hurt, or other emotions. The result can easily bring isolation and damage to the relationship—all the result of what was really a minor, mistaken comment. The antidote once again is the training we receive as disciples of the Lord. Set aside the loss to yourself and respond in love and charity. Pause and take time for discernment, asking what the truth of the situation is. Even if there was real malice behind the original comment, it derives from brokenness in your spouse that Jesus wants to heal. That's why we are instructed to pray for our enemies. Our enemy is not the person; it's the evil one at work in the brokenness afflicting the person.

Responding correctly with love and charity in situations like I have just described is not an easy thing. To be able to do it is one of the great fruits of Christian spiritual maturity. For one thing, it requires a great deal of self-discipline. If we ask ourselves how Jesus would respond, treating the situation as a matter for discernment rather than letting our emotions drive us to a shoot-from-the-hip response, things will work out much to the better. In walking the disciple's walk, following and serving Jesus, we become able to think like him and learn to perceive situations as he does. It is this training, this gift from the Holy Spirit, which enables us to respond in a manner that heals rather than aggravates the situation. Lastly, remember that training takes time. Jesus works with us gently over our entire lifetime. Be patient with yourself.

## Turning to Tradition

Human failings can be classified as 1) those that are evident to everyone, 2) those evident only to the person who has them, 3) those evident to everybody except the person who has them, and 4) those so hidden they are only evident to God. Sometime during the process of growing spiritually, in becoming fully healed and Christ-like, God will deal with all of these failings. In addition, God works in our innermost hearts to prepare us for the work he would have us do. These situations can cause protracted periods of spiritual struggle, lasting months and even years, and they arise early or late in the spiritual growth process. These are periods characterized by feelings of uncertainty, confusion, frustration, doubt, fear, etc. Absent are the "Consolations of God," as St. Ignatius of Loyola calls them—that sense of his nearness, love, and graces. When dealing with such a struggle, it is very important to keep in mind that it is only for a season and it will end. Still more importantly, God is with you through it all, as close as ever, even though you may not sense his presence.

The Church, as one might expect, has a great deal of accumulated wisdom in dealing with struggles like this. One very helpful resource is the tradition of seeing a "spiritual director." This should be a priest or someone trained in this ministry. However, it can also be helpful to consult with anyone whose spiritual maturity you admire and who is willing to engage in the relationship. The spiritual director's role is to aid people in discerning and understanding the facets of their particular struggle and to guide them on their spiritual journey. It may take more than one attempt to find the right spiritual director, but keep trying—it is worth the effort. The spiritual healing process virtually always involves bringing spiritual issues to the light where they can be understood and prayed for; a spiritual director can be invaluable for this. Conversely, trying to work through a struggle alone tends to keep things in the dark and is counterproductive.

Studying the lives of the saints is another resource the Church recommends. Even better than reading their biographies, personally I have found it more productive to study their own writings. The saints provide both encouragement to keep us going and understanding to help illumine our individual situations. Particularly classic is St. Ignatius of Loyola's *Rules for the Discernment of Spirits*, which is contained in one set of eight rules and another of fourteen. Used with prayer and contemplation, these "rules" give us an understanding of the spiritual struggles within us, godly and evil influences, and an indication of how best to discern and respond. Again, these are best used with the aid of a spiritual director. A much more recent and very helpful resource to uncover hidden obstacles and areas of brokenness is Linda Schubert's *Miracle Hour*, a guide to personal prayer. This forty-eight-page booklet covers twelve areas of prayer, including surrender, repentance, forgiveness, and Scripture reflections, in a way that enables the Holy Spirit to bring repressed problems to the light for healing.

**For Further Reflection**

- 1 Corinthians 12:10 to 13:13 — Key passages on love and the mystical body of Christ
- Psalm 91 — God desires healing for his people.
- *Miracle Hour: A Method of Prayer that Will Change Your Life* by Linda Schubert — It can be ordered from Miracles of the Heart Ministries, PO Box 4034, Santa Clara, CA 95056 or www.linda-schubert.com (also available in Spanish).
- *Rules for the Discernment of Spirits* by St. Ignatius of Loyola is available at http://www.discerninghearts.com/?page_id=1306.

## Chapter Ten

## <u>Closing Notes</u>

*Works of love are always a means of becoming closer to God.... Love in action is what gives us grace. (Mother Teresa[8])*

Did I say growing spiritually was fun? Okay, technically "joy-filled" would be a better term, but whatever. Living in unity with the Lord, working in response to the Holy Spirit, and then just watching the results open up before you *is* fun—fun in a deeply satisfying way. Paul describes the presence of the Holy Spirit as the pledge and down payment on our redemption, sort of a heavenly appetizer. I don't know how to say it better. Sometimes you just sit quietly, knowing the Lord is present with you. There is no communication in the sense of receiving information; there is just the sense of his presence. I'll always remember going to a party where everyone there was a committed Christian—and the Lord showed up and stayed for the whole thing. I think we all felt it. What a unique and wonderful experience that was! One thing you soon learn is that God *really* knows how to please his people.

One way to describe living in the Kingdom of God is that it elevates a person just ever so slightly above the secular world. It's like skating on ice; that very thin layer of water created by the pressure of blade on ice enables the skater to glide effortlessly across the ice. The separation is very small, almost undetectable, but the effect is great. Both a walker and a skater encounter the same bumps and irregularities of the ice (life), but the skater can glide over or past them, while the walker must struggle with each one. Obviously this is not a perfect analogy, but hopefully you get the point. In the world, everyone encounters the same difficulties, but the person living in harmony with the Holy Spirit is not affected in the same way. The

---

[8] *A Simple Path*, by Mother Teresa, compiled by Lucinda Vardey, Ballantine Books, Random House Publishing Group, 1995; p115 and back jacket cover

trouble does not penetrate quite as deep, and faith and hope bear their fruit.

## The Importance of Community

Community in one form or another is essential for the type of spiritual growth I have described in this book, a spiritual growth that takes place and flourishes in the real world, in and among real people. God's work is to draw all people to himself, and that means drawing them into community. "See how they love one another" describes this life in community. God is love, and that love must be manifested in the community of believers in order for others to see it, experience it, and be drawn into that love themselves.

The Holy Spirit blesses us in three ways:

- First, we become loving people, transformed by the Holy Spirit's work within us.
- Second, we find ourselves surrounded by loving people.
- Third, we seek to develop more loving people.

What a significant thing since in the end, it is love that endures. Whatever the difficulties you face, it is always easier to face them when God's love is present.

Not long ago the Lord sharpened my understanding of why his love is so closely tied to our role of servants and disciples. My wife couldn't sleep one night, so she got up and started reading a book, one of those romance novels she likes. After she had read for a while, she started to become sleepy, but she sensed that the Lord was urging her to continue reading. She realized there was something the Lord wanted her to see. Eventually she found it after skipping to the end of the book, where she read, "You can't find intimate love until you find friendship first."

This is the way God works, too. The deepest friendships develop with people you work with for a long time, where there is a common goal and a common commitment. You can see this in the military with "foxhole buddies," and I certainly experienced this in my career in aerospace when the tasks were often difficult and the hours long. In situations like these, you grow to deeply appreciate another person's gifts, commitment, and hard work.

Likewise, in the Christian walk and in the Christian community, when we engage in God's work we develop a deep appreciation of the Father, Jesus, and the Holy Spirit as persons. Through our direct and personal relationship, we learn we can have trust and confidence in God. We grow in admiration and awe at his wisdom and the passion of his love. The work to which he calls us becomes a work of love within us. Our experience within the community of believers reinforces and makes God's love more tangible. I have both seen and experienced this frequently among committed Christians, often in a very simple way. For example, when people are thinking about how God has helped them in the midst of a hard day, they will simply say, "How can people stand to live any other way?" The sense of gratitude is clear in their words and their voice. Life may be full of struggle, but if we walk as God's disciples, his love covers all.

**For Further Reflection**

- *Holy Spirit, Make Your Home in Me* by George T. Montague, SM, The Word Among Us Press, 2008.
- *Prayer* by Hans Urs von Balthasar, translation by Graham Harrison, Ignatius Press, 1986.

# About the Author

Dr. B. Jeffrey Anderson has served as teacher, organizer and speaker for church adult education, RCIA, Lenten missions and a variety of special programs in his parish and North Alabama for over thirty years. He and his wife, Beth, also a speaker and teacher, have been active in the Catholic Charismatic Renewal since 1972. They reside near Huntsville, Alabama. The Andersons have nine grown children and six grandchildren (still counting).

Until his retirement, Anderson worked for the National Aeronautics and Space Administration where he was regarded as one of the Agency's leading specialists on the effects of natural environment on aerospace systems. His work contributed to the Space Shuttle, International Space Station, Chandra Telescope and the Constellation Program which began work to return man to the moon and then on to Mars. Dr. Anderson holds a Ph.D. in Physics from the University of Nevada, Reno.

Made in the USA
Charleston, SC
26 November 2014